MTN

Flower Watch

A guide to the Cape's floral wonders

PETER JOYCE

WESTERN CAPE TOURISM

Struik Publishers (Pty) Ltd
(A member of the Struik New Holland Publishing Group)
Cornelis Struik House
80 McKenzie Street
Cape Town
8001

Reg. No. 54/00965/07

2 4 6 8 10 9 7 5 3 1

First published 1999

Butterfly Aeropetes tulbaghia *pollinating* Erica mammosa

Designer: Janice Evans
Project manager: Pippa Parker
Editorial team: Peter Joyce, Giséle Raad, Judy Bryant
Design assistant: Illana Fridkin
Indexer and proofreader: Claudia Dos Santos
Consultants: Lynette Heydenrych (MTN) and
Elsabet Muller (Western Cape Tourism Board)
Picture researcher: Carmen Watts
Cartographer: Elaine Fick

Reproduction by Hirt & Carter (Pty) Ltd., Cape Town

Printed and bound by:
CTP Book Printers (Pty) Ltd, Cape Town

ISBN: 1 86872 304 6

The publishers wish to thank the following for their
courteous co-operation in the preparation of this book:
MTN, the Western Cape Tourism Board, and the tourism
authorities of Namaqualand, the West Coast (including
Olifants River Valley, Swartland and Sandveld), the Cape
Metropolitan area, the Cape Winelands, the Breede River
Valley, Klein Karoo Kannaland, and the Garden Route.

Front cover: Clanwilliam Wildflower Garden
Title page: Cyrtanthus elatus in the Robinson Pass
Back cover (top to bottom, from left to right): Butterfly Aloeides
thyra *on* Pseudoselago serrata; *Erica mammosa; Pincushion;*
Sparaxis, *Nieuwoudtville*
Spine: Nieuwoudtville Bulbinella

Orange-breasted sunbird on
Liparia splendens

Contents

Foreword

WESTERN CAPE TOURISM

The Western Cape boasts the most diverse floral heritage in the world. Fully sixty-eight per cent of the 8 600 species that grow in the Cape Floral Kingdom can be found nowhere else on earth. No wonder botanists and flower lovers have recognized the region as one of the finest of all international destinations!

Different species flower throughout the year in the Cape Floral Kingdom, but the peak period – between August and September – offers breathtaking vistas of vast carpets of flowers, wonderfully rich in their colour and variety. We extend a warm invitation to you to come and experience this unparalleled botanical splendour. We are geared to making your visit an unforgettable one.

The Western Cape Tourism Board is proud of its association with MTN. This partnership in tourism has been a rewarding one for everyone, and especially for the many people who work within the industry.

I therefore have no doubt that this publication, with its extensive coverage of the Cape Floral Kingdom, will become an invaluable, if not the definitive, source of information of its kind, and draw even more visitors from all over South Africa and the world.

While you are in our province, make a point of experiencing the culture of our people and our state-of-the-art tourism infrastructure.

Enjoy your visit to 'Africa's fairest Cape'!

DR MIKE FABRICIUS
Chief Executive Officer
Western Cape Tourism Board

Sponsor's Foreword

Each year, between August and September, the Cape dons a floral jacket that draws thousands of people, both local and international tourists, to the remote corners of the Cape Floral Kingdom. The region, indeed, has become synonymous with natural beauty and splendour.

The Cape's unpredictable weather, and especially its infamously hot berg winds, determines the nature of the flower season, which varies in its timing, duration and locality from year to year. However, the MTN Flowerline, in conjunction with the Western Cape Tourism Board, strives to provide accurate and up-to-date information on where the flowers are to be seen at their best at any given time – a practical, at times almost essential service to all those enthusiasts who set out in search of the glorious floral shows.

At MTN we firmly believe in the responsible management and utilization of natural resources. Our flagship environmental project, the MTN Cape Whale Route, recently won the prestigious British Airways Tourism for Tomorrow Awards for responsible and sustainable ecotourism. The Route encompasses MTN's support of several other projects such as Seawatch, the Black Oystercatcher Conservation Programme and efforts to save the endangered African (jackass) penguin. Public education and accessible information is the key to the success of these and all other conservation efforts, and we believe that MTN *Flower Watch* will contribute to making your excursion a satisfying and enriching one while, at the same time, helping relieve some of the pressure which is placed on this fragile floral extravaganza every year.

Peter During
Regional General Manager: MTN

Introduction

*T*his book is designed as a simple guide to the flowering plants of the Cape Floral Kingdom and of Namaqualand, regions world-famed for the beauty and variety of their flora.

The coverage is by no means comprehensive: several large volumes would be needed to do full justice to all the families, genera and species that grow in these remarkable botanical zones. *Flower Watch* has more modest intent: it focuses on those places that are most likely to prove rewarding to the flower hunter, and illuminates some of their more common and colourful plants. The eight chapters, each embracing a coherent tourist area, are arranged in geographical order, starting with Namaqualand in the north and ending with the coast and hinterland of the lovely Garden Route in the east. Each has been written, to some extent, with the general traveller as well the plant enthusiast in mind – on the assumption that the latter, however keen, won't want to spend every moment of their visit in search of flowers.

TIMES AND PLACES

Namaqualand and the West Coast are the best known, most popular destinations: for a few springtime weeks their annuals put on a quite dazzling show, covering the otherwise rather dull plains and hillsides in a riot of colour. Some hints:

The weather varies; the winter rains may be early or late, modest or generous; some parts of the region will get more rain than others, and it falls at different times in different places. Moreover, a hot berg (or mountain) wind can wilt a vast carpet of lovely blooms within a day or two. So it's difficult to predict just when and where one can see the displays at their best. Contact the MTN Flowerline (see box) before setting out.

The flowers open during the hottest parts of the day (from about 11 am to 4 pm), and turn their faces to the sun. They are best viewed, therefore, by driving or walking with the sun behind you. They remain closed on very overcast days.

The flowering season begins earlier in the Namaqualand's northern areas, advancing into the West Coast region with the warmer weather. Thus it would be sensible to start your trip – if it's an extended one – from the Springbok area and slowly make your way south.

Those with less time to spare (and who prefer not to go it alone) have numerous coach excursions to choose from. Options range from day trips to three-day and even longer tours. Contact the Western Cape Tourism Board or Cape Town's Tourism Gateway Centre for the details (see box).

The Cape's floral wonders, though, are by no means confined to Namaqualand and the West Coast. The fynbos of the Cape Peninsula, and of the lands that stretch north across the Winelands to the Breede River valley and eastwards to the Tsitsikamma area, is quite remarkable for the wealth of its flowering plants. Part of the Overberg, for example, was recently registered by UNESCO as a 'biosphere reserve' in an international bid to conserve its extraordinarily rich flora. The flowers of the fynbos biome tend to be less obvious than those of the western regions; they don't mass together in quite so spectacular a fashion; many are uncommon, some are rare, and one must search for them. But you'll invariably find the effort well worth while. Moreover, although there are peak flowering periods in the various fynbos areas, there is no closed season: whatever the time of year, you will see at least some of the plants in bloom.

INFORMATION

A good place to learn something about the region's floral heritage is Kirstenbosch National Botanical Garden, on the eastern slopes of Table Mountain (see page 37). Here, thousands of indigenous plant species are on show within a relatively small area, and they provide a splendid overview of what you can expect to see on your wider travels.

For up-to-date information on the best places in the region to see the flowers at a given time, contact the MTN FLOWERLINE on (toll-free) 083 910 1028. The service is available on weekdays from July to October.

Alternatively, call in at Cape Town Tourism, Pinnacle Building, corner of Burg and Castle streets, tel (021) 426 4267/8 or 426 4260; fax (021) 426 4266. The building also houses the Western Cape Tourism Board. These offices, and the various regional bureaus (see page 94), will also recommend destinations, and provide you with information on routes, tours and accommodation.

The Region's Flowers

The floral wealth of the Cape coastal belt and the hillsides and mountains of the hinterland rank among the wonders of the botanical world. Nowhere else will you find such a concentrated diversity of flowering plants.

The area covered in this book extends from the sandy plains and mountains of Namaqualand southwards, around the Cape of Good Hope and then east to the green and pleasant Tsitsikamma – together comprising a segment of the country which, for the most part, is subject to summer droughts, whose sandstone and quartzite soils are poor in nutrients, and whose plants are hardy, highly adapted and often exquisitely beautiful. They are also remarkably different from those found elsewhere in South Africa, indeed anywhere else on earth.

So special is this floral wonderland – which is just 90 000 km² in extent, occupying less that 0.5 per cent of the earth's land surface, or just under 4 per cent of southern Africa – that it has been classed as one of the world's six Floral Kingdoms. The latter are botanical regions based on the number of endemic plant families, genera and species (that is, plants that grow naturally nowhere else) they support; the Cape kingdom is by far the smallest of all, but it nevertheless enjoys equal status with the others, including that which encompasses North America, Europe and most of Asia.

The eastern end of False Bay is dominated by the heights of the Hottentots Holland range. Beyond lies the flower-rich Overberg.

The Cape Floral Kingdom is home to nearly 9 000 species, or a phenomenal 1 300 per 10 000 km². About 20 per cent of the genera, and 68 per cent of the species, are endemic. Six entire families – the Penaeaceae, Grubbiaceae, Stilbaceae, Roridulaceae, Geissolomaceae and the Retziaceae – are unique to the area. Only one species of a seventh family, the Bruniaceae, grows elsewhere.

The Cape Flora is made up of several different types of vegetation, most of it shrubland of one kind or another. To summarize briefly:

FYNBOS. The best known of the shrublands, fynbos covers the sandy, infertile soils of the Cape lowlands and mountains. It has four major components, namely the grass- or reed-like restioids (family Restionaceae; the proteoids (Proteaceae)) with their large leathery leaves; the ericoids, which have small, heath-type leaves and belong to a number of plant families including the Ericaceae; and finally bulbs and bulb-like plants.

Less numerous (about 370 species in 13 genera) but enormously varied are the proteas, named after the Greek god who could change his shape at will. The genus *Protea* itself (117 species) has closely grouped, needle-shaped flowers that grow closely together to form a compact head, surrounded by brightly coloured bracts which envelop and sometimes hide the flowers. Among the more familiar members of the family are the king protea (South Africa's national flower), which has the largest flowerhead of all, and the tall waboom or wagon tree. Other genera include the leucospermums, popularly known as pincushions; and leucadendrons which include, among much else, an array of red- and yellow-tipped bushes and the graceful silver tree (see page 37). On the western coastal plain there is sandveld fynbos, which is a sparser shrubland.

RENOSTERVELD. This vegetation type is related to (though much less well known than) fynbos. It's a shrubland that grows on the richer clayey soils of the Cape forelands, and comprises for the most part small-leafed ericoid plants, most notably the rather dull grey shrub called rhinoceros bush or renosterbos (*Elytropappus rhinocerotis*). You won't find many proteas in the renosterveld, and practically no restios, but the bulbs – especially the lilies, irises and amaryllids – are spectacular in their season. Much of the renosterveld has been replaced by the wheat and other cropfields of the Swartland and Overberg, but it survives on land which has not or cannot be ploughed.

STRANDVELD (not to be confused with 'sandveld', which is not a vegetation type but a geographical region: the western coastal plain). Also a shrubland, strandveld is found on the sandy soils of western seaboard's ancient marine beds. The shrubs – such as salie or sage – bear medium-sized leaves and many of them, sustained by the slightly more nutrient-rich coastal sands, are able to produce berries. Prominent among these is the bietou bush (*Chrysanthemoides monilifera*). In between the shrubs are bare, sandy patches which host a myriad annuals. These establish themselves with the early autumn rains to reach their glorious flowering peak by early spring.

SUCCULENT KAROO. These low, sparse succulent-leafed shrublands cover all of Namaqualand and the dry reaches of the Klein (or Little) Karoo. Most notable are the vygies or mesembs (family Mesembryanthemaceae; see page 18).

FORESTS. The largest of the indigenous forests cover extensive parts of the Knysna area in the east, though they also flourish in moist or fire-protected ravines on most of the Cape's mountains. The Langeberg, Outeniqua and Tsitsikamma ranges sustain a splendid array of ironwoods, stinkwoods, giant yellowwoods and other handsome high-canopy tree species.

Just why so many different plants thrive in so small an area as the Cape Floral Kingdom is still not fully understood. In all probability, though, changes in climate over millions of years, frequent fires, the broken terrain and a variety of nutrient-poor soils created a huge range of habitats, encouraging the plants to evolve in new ways.

CONSERVING THE LEGACY

As with so much of the world's natural heritage, Cape flora is under severe pressure. Much of the region's original vegetation has disappeared beneath plough and pasture; among major and continuing threats are the invasion of water-guzzling aliens (notably Australian wattles) and the consequent erosion, urban sprawl, coastal tourism and leisure development, the harvesting of wild flowers, and too-frequent veld fires.

Much of the Cape's precious mountain vegetation is protected within sanctuaries of one sort or another. These fulfil a vital function, of course, and the creation of 'biosphere reserves', which are designed to maintain a workable balance between the human and natural worlds, holds promise for the more threatened areas. Intelligent veld management and a sensible approach to ecotourism – both of which demand political will and a fresh look at funding – can do much to keep degradation at bay. The long-term future, however, can be ensured only if the majority of ordinary people become aware of the value of their flora, and commit themselves to safeguarding it.

Lüderitz

Orange

Port Nolloth

Springbok

NAMAQUALAND

GREAT KAROO

Nieuwoudtville

Strandveld: part of the western coastal region, but not extensive enough to feature on this map

☐ Succulent Karoo

☐ Fynbos

☐ Forest

Lambert's Bay

• Beaufort West

WEST COAST

Saldanha

WINELANDS

KLEIN KAROO

GARDEN ROUTE

Breede

George

Port Elizabeth

Cape Town

OVERBERG

CAPE PENINSULA

Succulent karoo vegetation as seen in the Klein Karoo.

Typical succulent karoo vegetation in Namaqualand.

Fynbos

Forest

Namaqualand

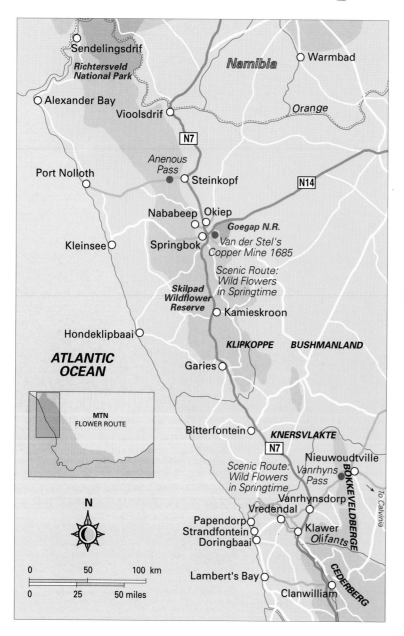

For most of the year much of Namaqualand – all but the southern parts – looks bone-dry, its landscapes dun-coloured, bleak, with little to please the eye, the great silent spaces seemingly empty of all but the toughest of living forms. Yet this is one of the great treasure-houses of the botanical world, haven to more than 3 000 different floral species, many of which, for a few weeks in springtime, burst into riotous life, clothing the countryside in a spectacular mantle of orange, yellow and white blooms. The region, nearly all of which falls within the Northern Cape province, is not precisely defined (it has no formal boundaries), but is generally taken to cover the roughly 100-km strip of terrain running along the country's west coast, from the Vanrhynsdorp area near the Olifants River to the lower reaches of the Orange River in the north. It is sparsely populated, the largest of its few urban centres the dusty little town of Springbok, on the main N7 highway and 555 km from Cape Town.

THE WILD FLOWERS

The most immediately striking of Namaqualand's plants are the annuals, highly adapted desert emphemerals which germinate quickly, growing and flowering in an explosion of colour after good winter rains. These are most often to be found on overgrazed veld, or on formerly ploughed lands that have been abandoned (known as 'oldfields') and in fallow (unplanted) fields. In all these areas the natural vegetation has been destroyed and then colonized by pioneer species, many growing from wind-borne seeds blown in from afar. Precisely where, when and for how long these flowers put on their show, though, varies hugely from season to season. And the displays are precarious: a hot, untimely berg or mountain wind that blows in from the interior can wilt a massive carpet of blooms in just one day. Contact the MTN Flowerline (see box, page 5) for the most up-to-date information.

Apart from these instantly accessible, dazzling tapestries of bright spring colour, Namaqualand sustains a wide variety of perennials: geophytes (bulb-like plants), dwarf shrubs and a huge number of succulents, some ground-creeping, a few of tree height. These veld plants are often more established and withstand unfavourable conditions better than the annuals, and though generally less obvious, have their own beauty. The flowers of many vygie shrubs (Mesembryanthemaceae), for example, have an eye-catching, jewel-like intensity of colour.

All of the region's plants are highly adapted to survive the long summer dryness. Some of those growing near the coast depend for their moisture on the nighttime mists that often roll in from the cool Atlantic Ocean. Succulents store water in their fleshy

Wild flowers on view in the Goegap Nature Reserve near Springbok. Other prominent elements of the rugged countryside include the kokerboom trees and huge, rounded granite boulders.

Above: *Dense patches of golden-hued* Bulbinella latifolia *garland parts of the Nieuwoudtville Wild Flower Reserve in August and September.*
Below: *The charming little bat-eared fox, which feeds on insects, rodents and fruit, is a resident of the richly endowed Goegap reserve.*

leaves and stems; the leaves of the geophytes lie flat on the ground, creating their own microclimate; some shrubs with medium-sized leaves shed them during the hot, dry months to minimize transpiration (water loss). The annuals play a waiting game: their seeds lie dormant in the dry earth, sometimes for years, until the rains come.

THE NATURE OF THE LAND

Namaqualand can be divided, according to the nature of the rocks, soils, vegetation and other elements, into a number of fairly distinct environments.

The sandveld stretches across the westerly coastal plain and is covered mainly in what is known as strandveld, short vegetation embracing vygies and taller shrubs such as skil-padbos (*Zygophyllum morgsana*). Among the shrubs are good shows of apricot-to-cerise volstruisvygie flowers. In the sandveld, too – from Kleinsee southwards – are wind-blown patches that support fynbos, notably the sandveld pincushion (whose leaves are densely covered with short, silvery-grey hairs) and fields of reed-like restoids.

In the south-central interior, between Vanrhynsdorp and Bitterfontein, lies the Knersvlakte, a vast, desolate-looking land of gently rolling hills, flattish plains and quartz fields that look barren but which are in fact studded with miniature stone plants. In between are reddish soils that sustain low shrubs and vygies (for instance, the creeping *Cephalophyllum*). Springtime brings out the annuals; and heuweltjies – termite mounds of ancient origin – are bright with yellow perdeblom. To the north of the Knersvlakte is the Klipkoppe, a rockier, rugged land of huge granite domes. This is part of the wider Hardeveld, an area covered by vegetation known as Namaqualand Broken Veld – a reference to the way tall, scattered plants break the monotony of the low shrublands. Here you'll find many succulent shrubs (notably vygies), euphorbias, the highly palatable perdebos, taller evergreen shrubs such as *Ozoroa* (or resin trees), witgatbos, klipvy and Namaqua fig. The better watered Kamiesberg nurtures renosterveld enlivened by spectacular bulbs in spring and autumn; fynbos grows on the highest peaks.

Farther east, towards Nieuwoudtville and the Bokkeveld escarpment, rainfall increases dramatically and there are marked changes in both geology and soil. The nutrient-poor sandstone soils at the edge of the escarpment support dry mountain fynbos, conspicuous among which is *Protea laurifolia*, the grey-leafed sugarbush with its cream to silvery flowerhead bearing a brown beard. Nearer Nieuwoudtville are the shales that sustain renosterbos, wild rosemary and a

Argyroderma fissum, vingervygie. Family Mesembryanthemaceae. A miniature succulent, growing to less than 20 cm in height and found on the quartz fields of the Knersvlakte. Its flowers are produced in midwinter.

Aloe krapohliana. Family Asphodelaceae. This tiny aloe (30 cm tall) is quite a rare plant, occurring from Knersvlakte to Alexander Bay. Its leaf rosette is about 15 cm in diameter.

Phyllobolus digitatus, fingers-and-thumbs. Family Mesembryanthemaceae. A miniature succulent growing to less than 25 cm in height on the quartz fields of the Knersvlakte. The flowers are produced in December.

Lachenalia framesii, viooltjie. Family Hyacinthaceae. This plant, endemic to the Knersvlakte, has yellowish flowers with strikingly contrasting magenta tips. It is found in large colonies in the flat, sandy areas of the Knersvlakte. Flowers in late winter (July–August).

Crassula columnaris, sentkannetjie. Family Crassulaceae. This miniature succulent grows to about 10 cm in height. It is found widely in Namaqualand as well as in the quartz fields of the Knersvlakte.

Moraea deserticola, uintjie. Family Iridaceae. Also a Knersvlakte endemic, found on shale soils. The plant produces its flowers in spring.

Babiana sp. bobbejaantjie. Family Iridaceae. A newly discovered and hence as yet unnamed species. Found only on limestone outscrops in the Knersvlakte. Cerise with some yellow streaks on the flower parts. The plant usually flowers in early spring (August).

Monilaria moniliformis. Family Mesembryanthemaceae. A low succulent whose winter leaves disappear in summer, leaving erect, jointed, brown stems resembling strings of beads. It occurs on quartz and rocky sites in the Knersvlakte and on rocks near the coast. Spring flowering.

Namaqualand in springtime. The region sustains an astonishing 3 000 and more flowering plants, the most immediately striking of which are the annuals that appear en masse after good winter rains.

feathery grass. Inland still and one finds doleritic soil and a special vegetation that includes a stunning array of bulbs (among them the lynx tail or rooikatstert, with its deep orange-red spikes), some of them found nowhere else in the world. Beyond lies the rather isolated little town of Calvinia and the Nama Karoo.

Finally, there is the far north's Richtersveld, a rugged and remote mountain desert enclave sprawling within a great loop of the Orange River.

THE SOUTHERN AREAS

Vanrhynsdorp is a pleasant little town, well served by guesthouses (it also boasts restaurants, two museums and a wine route) and a convenient base from which to explore the flowers of the sandveld coastal area to the west, the Knersvlakte to the north, the

Calendar

Namaqualand's flowering season is fickle, the weather determining where and when the blooms are at their most eye-catching. The season tends to start and end earlier in the north, especially in the Richtersveld. Flowering is later along the foggy coast, and in the cooler, wetter Kamiesberge on the Bokkeveld plateau. Contact Flowerline (see below right) for the best times and places.

SPRING: The peak season, with annuals, bulb-like plants, shrubs, vygies, and daisies combining to create a glorious display.

SUMMER: The strange halfmens tree might attract visitors to the Richtersveld, but bear in mind the searing heat of the season.

AUTUMN: The most enchanting flowers are those of miniature stone-plants growing on quartz fields – bababoudjies (*Argyroderma*) and, in the rock crevices, dumplings (*Conophytum*). In mid-to late March the Nieuwoudtville area offers dazzling fields of amaryllids such as maartblom

A kokerboom, or quiver tree, stands in solitary splendour on the plains of the Richtersveld.

(*Brunsvigia bosmaniae*), geelsambreelblom (*Crossyne flava*), kwaslelie (*Boophone haemanthoides*), the river lily (*Crinum variabile*) and *Haemanthus* species.

WINTER: Highlights are the aloes, including the yellow-orange spires of *Aloe framesii*. Some vygies start to produce flowers in late winter. Annuals begin their displays in the north from mid-June.

For up-to-date information, call the MTN Flowerline 083 910 1028 (June to October).

FLORAL HIGHLIGHTS: NAMAQUALAND

Cephalophyllum spongiosum, volstruisvygie. Family Mesembryanthemaceae. A low, sprawling succulent shrublet, characteristic of Namaqualand strandveld. One of the earliest plants to flower, its large, brilliant blooms appear in midwinter and last through to spring.

Aloe dichotoma, kokerboom or quiver tree. Family Asphodelaceae. This tall (5–6m) tree is widespread in the arid western region of southern Africa. The hollow stems were used by Bushmen as receptacles for arrows, hence the common name. Flowers appear in winter.

Oxalis obtusa, suring, sorrel. Family Oxalidaceae. A very low (up to 10 cm) plant with 3–5 leaflets. Widespread in Namaqualand and into the southwestern Cape, Karoo and into Namibia. Flowers in a range of colours – pink, red, yellow, white – are produced in July–October.

Gazania krebsiana, botterblom. Family Asteraceae. A low, tufted perennial shrublet found on flats and low slopes and on roadsides. The flowers, ranging from yellow to orange, appear in spring in Namaqualand, but at other times elsewhere in southern Africa.

Babiana curviscapa, perde-uintjie. Family Iridaceae. A perennial bulb-like plant that grows up to 20 cm in height on Namaqualand's sandy flats from Garies to Steinkopf. Its leaves are ribbed and hairy. The flowers, which are magenta to purple with a white throat, are produced in late July–September.

Lapeirousia silenoides, meidestert. Family Iridaceae. This bulb-like plant, up to 25 cm tall, grows on granite, on coarse granite soils and in rocky places (often in rocky crevices) in Namaqualand between Garies and Springbok. Its magenta to cerise flowers, with cream markings, appear late July–September.

Gladiolus equitans, Namaqua kalkoentjie. Family Iridaceae. A bulb-like plant whose broad leaves form a fan. Found on granite soils from Knersvlakte to the mountains around Springbok. Its orange to scarlet flowers are produced in late August to mid-September.

FLORAL HIGHLIGHTS: NAMAQUALAND

Lachenalia splendida. Family Hyacinthaceae. This bulb, which grows to 25 cm in height, produces only two leaves at any one time. It occurs in the sandy flats of the Knersvlakte. The pale lilac flowers appear July–August.

Dimorphotheca curveata. Family Asteraceae. This woody perennial shrublet, up to 60 cm tall, grows on sandy gravel on flats and lower slopes from Kamieskroon to Karoopoort and Touws River. The flowers are white with purple-brown on the reverse, and less frequently orange-yellowish. Flowers August–September.

Hoodia gordonia, ghaap. Family Asclepiadaceae. An upright, many-angled succulent with branches up to 45 cm and bearing spines. Grows in both dry rocky areas and on sandy river beds. Pale purple flowers appear (mostly) in November–January.

Euphorbia mauritanica, bees-melkbos. Family Euphorbiaceae. A shrub, 1–1.5 m in height, that consists of many upright succulent branches. It is widely distributed throughout the drier parts of southern Africa. The yellow flowers are produced August–October.

Cheiridopsis robusta. Family Mesembryanthemaceae. A low, clump-forming plant with fat, paired, succulent leaves emerging from papery sleeves. Found mostly on quartz fields, but also in granite, from Richtersveld to Kamieskroon. Yellow to cream to salmon flowers are produced in June–September.

Lachenalia pallida. Family Hyacinthaceae. A bulb that grows to 10–25 cm in height around Malmesbury, Stellenbosch and the Saldanha area. The white to pale yellow flowers are produced August–October.

Tripteris oppositifolia, skaapbos. Family Asteraceae. This shrub, 0.5–1m tall, occurs on sandy flats in Namaqualand and farther afield, to Nieuwoudtville and the Karoo. The yellow or orange flowers appear in July–October.

A WONDERLAND OF VYGIES

Namaqualand is home to a huge number of mesembryanthemums or vygies – in fact, to most of the world's 2 000-plus species (which makes it South Africa's largest plant family), with more to be discovered. They range from creeping ground covers and miniature stone plants to round bushes growing to nearly half a metre in height, varying hugely in size, hue, form and habitat, many of them bringing dazzling springtime brilliance to the region's otherwise bleak plains and hillsides. Their flowers are daisy-like, showy, with brilliant shiny petals ranging in colour from white and yellow through the pinks to scarlet and vermilion.

One of the first mesembryanthemums found by the early European collectors was a suurvy (*Carpobrotus*), a member of the only group to have fleshy fruit – hence the name vygie, or fig. The rest of the family have non-fleshy fruits, which can be papery to hard. These hold the seeds until the first rains prompt the multi-sectioned lid to open and release their contents, in some cases by means of complex mechanisms. On drying, the lid closes again to protect the remaining seeds. Wet the capsule and watch it happen. Among the more widely cultivated mesembryanthemums are the vygie miniatures or stone plants; *Drosanthemum*, commonly known as the dew flower because of its lustrous leaves; the Livingstone daisy; *Lampranthus* (shining flower), and the trailing *Carpobrotus* (sour fig).

Lampranthus

Argyroderma crateriforme

Drosanthemum hispidum

Olifants River valley and the splendidly rugged Matsikamma, Gifberg and Cederberg mountains (see next chapter, page 22) in the south. The local succulent nursery, large and well stocked, is well worth a visit. A succulent trail (apparently the only one in the world) leads through the pebbly hills and red-sand plains of the Knersvlakte.

Even more rewarding (usually) is the road northeast, the R27 from Vanrhynsdorp towards the Bokkeveldberg, up Vanrhyn's Pass (there are fine views over the coastal terrace) to Nieuwoudtville and beyond, to the western Karoo (or, rather more correctly perhaps, Bushmanland) town of Calvinia. This is a lonely corner of the country – author Laurens van der Post wrote of 'farms hidden behind rare puritanical hills guarding secret water, so that [the land] appears totally unpeopled' – but it's a visual joy in early spring. Among venues of special note are the Nieuwoudtville Wild Flower Reserve and its spectacular bulbs (*Bulbinella* and *Romulea*, or satynblomme and frutangs), kalossies (*Ixia*), sysies (*Geissorhiza*, among them the endemic blue pride of Nieuwoudtville) – a kaleidoscope of colour in season. The Oorlogskloof Nature Reserve, 18 km to the south of Nieuwoudtville, merits a special excursion for its rugged scenery, its restios, its massed flowers of attractive bruingannabos (*Passerina glomerata*) and its sugarbushes.

Calvinia's Akkerdam Nature Reserve, set beneath the Hantam range, provides sanctuary for an array of birds and game animals, and is a floral delight during the spring months, boasting, among its many other treasures, the snowy-white, magenta-centred blooms of the karoosneeu (*Dorotheanthus maughanii*).

THE ROAD TO SPRINGBOK

The main highway continues north through the rugged countryside and its lonely little farming settlements, most prominent of which are Garies and Kammieskroon (the hotel here is a popular base for flower-hunters), both girded by granite hills, the countryside sustaining shrubby vygies, yellow daisy bushes, patches of taller shrubs such as taaibos (*Rhus*), bulbs, berggousblom (*Ursinia*), gousblom (*Arctotis*) and other annuals.

To the north of Kamieskroon you'll see tall kokerboom trees (*Aloe dichotoma*) whose yellow, candle-like flowers appear in late winter. Just to the west of town is the Skilpad Wildflower Reserve, once a farm whose abandoned fields are now rich in springtime wild flowers, most of them comprising berggousblom mixed here and there with teebossie (*Leysera tenella*), sambreeltjies (*Felicia australis*) and sporries (*Heliophila*). The unploughed areas support a variety of bulbs and wild geraniums.

The first Dutch settlers took a keen interest in what they called the 'copper mountains' of the Springbok area (a rather fruitless expedition was dispatched as early 1685), but it wasn't until the mid-19th century that serious attempts were made to extract the metal. Lively little mining settlements grew up around the workings at Okiep, Nababeep and Carolusberg. Springbok itself started life in earlier, rather quieter times to become a fairly substantial farming centre that now serves as the region's commercial and administrative headquarters – and, in late winter and springtime, as something of a mecca for flower enthusiasts. In good years the area's floral displays are quite breathtaking.

Fifteen kilometres to the east is the Goegap Nature Reserve, a 15 000-ha expanse of rough, beautiful terrain dominated by huge, dome-like granite hillocks. Plant life, still classified as Namaqualand Broken Veld, includes succulents (the kokerboom trees are notable) and a glory of spring flowers; among the reserve's 45 or so mammal species are klipspringer, springbok, Hartmann's mountain zebra and the bat-eared fox. Vehicle and walking trails have been laid out.

THE FAR NORTH

The road that branches off from the N7 to the west (at Steinkopf, a little more than 50 km beyond Springbok) leads you through ever more arid

Brunsvigia bosmaniae, maartblom. Family Amaryllidaceae. A large bulb with bright pink tubular flowers, scented like narcissus, borne at the end of long stalks in March–May. Dried flowerheads tumble across the veld dispersing seed. Found on clay soils on rocky outcrops.

Sparaxis tricolor, harlequin flower. Family Iridaceae. A bulb-like plant, 10–30 cm tall, found along streams in damp, clayey soil on the Bokkeveld escarpment (where it is an endemic, listed in the Red Data Book). Orange flowers with yellow and black cups appear September–October.

Geissorhiza splendidissima, blue pride of Nieuwoudtville. Family Iridaceae. This bulb-like plant, up to 20 cm tall, grows on clayey flats among stones near Nieuwoudtville on the Bokkeveld escarpment, where it is endemic. Dark-blue glossy flowers with black throat appear late August–September.

Romulea sabulosa, satynblom. Family Iridaceae. A bulb-like plant, up to 10 cm tall, that grows in clayey soil in renosterveld on the Bokkeveld escarpment, to which it is endemic. Glossy red flowers (satin-like, hence the common name) appear July–September.

For a brief period each year the landscapes around Springbok, on the main north-south highway, are a glorious riot of colour, much of it conferred by yellow daisy bushes and magenta vygies.

countryside, and down the Anenous Pass to the little seaboard town of Port Nolloth. To the south, at the mouth of the Buffels River, is Kleinsee, which is smaller, even more remote (although a good road, the R355, connects the village with Springbok). Desolate though these sandveld wastelands appear, they too have their floral season.

Port Nolloth was born to serve the copper mines of the interior but took on a new role when diamonds were discovered, in 1925, on the coastal strip running up to the Orange River. Diggers converged from all corners of the country, and indeed from much farther afield; a few fortunes were made (one man, the geologist Hans Merensky, found nearly 500 stones beneath a single flat rock) and for a time the area was the focus of frenetic and sometimes unruly activity. In due course, however, the government moved in, declaring the area to be state diggings. The town is much quieter now, though its residents, and the concession divers who arrive to work the offshore gravels, are known for their sociability. Alexander Bay, near the Orange River mouth and accessible via a rather rough coastal road, is the hub of Namaqualand's alluvial diamond industry, and a tour of the diggings, animated and noisy with huge earth-movers, is a memorable experience. Tours are conducted on Thursdays. In springtime the strandveld inland is ablaze with the colours of pietsnot (*Grielum*), reenblommetjie (*Dimorphotheca pluvialis*), Namaqualand daisies, vygies such as volstruisvygie, the large white flowers of t'noutsiama (*Cheiridopsis denticulata*) and other plants.

Inland to the north of Alexander Bay are the plains and hills and stark rock formations of the Richtersveld, a wild, harsh and, much of it, hauntingly beautiful 'mountain desert' that draws serious botanists and the keener hiker and camper. Just over 160 000 ha of the wilderness is a proclaimed national park, established to conserve the area's unique scenery and flora and administered in terms of a contractual arrangement with the local stock farmers. The area is famed for its plant life: the flora is largely succulent – strange halfmens and kokerbooms (or quiver trees) stand guard over parts of the bleak landscape; about a third of all known mesembryanthemum species are found on the broad, lonely acres (see box, page 18). *Aloe pillansii*, *A. ramosissima* and the summer-flowering *A. pearsonii* (in the higher reaches) are among the aloes; *Euphorbia decussata* and *E. dregeana* among the euphorbias.

Below: *The strange-looking halfmens ('half-man') or elephant's trunk tree grows in the desolate reaches of the far north. The Afrikaans name derives from an early Nama belief that trees were human beings magically transformed into plants.*
Below left: Grielum *in glorious flower in the Garies area.*
Bottom: *The wreck of a small boat near the fishing harbour of Port Nolloth.*

The West Coast

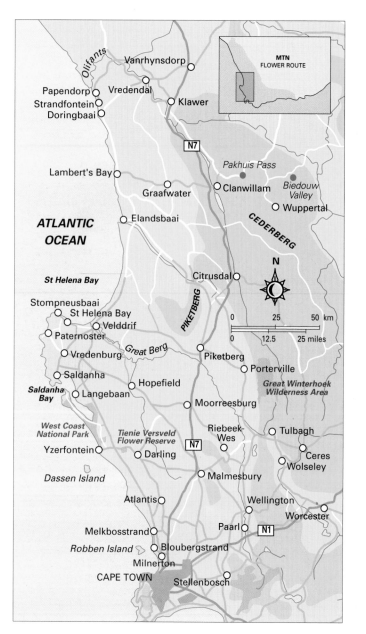

The land that stretches north from Cape Town, along the Atlantic seaboard and eastwards, across the flattish coastal plain to the grand heights of the Cederberg, beckons the flower enthusiast: in late winter and, especially, in springtime the land is transfigured by patches and in places great carpets of wild blooms.

Broadly speaking the West Coast region supports four different types of vegetation:

◆ Along a fairly wide strip of coastal terrain you'll find strandveld: shrublands of gwarrie (*Euclea*), salie (*Salvia*), showy daisies (especially bietou) and other clumped plants thrive on the coarse sands and dunes. In some places, notably near Langebaan, outcrops of granite and limestone produce endemics such as *Muraltia harveyana* and fascinating miniature succulent gardens.

◆ Farther inland are the reed-like restios of the sandveld fynbos and, somewhat less prominent, proteas and ericas (very few of the latter). Daisy bushes and scrophs – members of the Scrophulariaceceae – are an attractive springtime feature; look out for *Zaluzianskya* and *Hebenstretia robusta*.

◆ Beyond the coastal plain – on the richer clayey soils of the Swartland – are the generally rather dull shrublands of the renosterveld and some spectacular bulbs, but much of the countryside has been cleared for crops and there is very little of the natural vegetation left. A special form of renosterveld survives around the town of Darling, where eroded granite has created islands of more fertile soil, producing a fine complement of bulbs and the bright blooms of kelkiewyn and bobbejaantjie (*Babiana rubrocyanea*).

◆ Finally, the slopes and heights of the Cederberg are mantled in typical mountain fynbos, the plant life a mix of proteas, ericas and restios.

The charms of the West Coast, though, extend well beyond its floral interest. The countryside has its scenic splendours, the country towns, each with its own history and distinctive personality, are both attractive and hospitable; the shoreline and its kelp-scented fishing villages beckon the bird-spotter and whale-watcher (the coast is a rewarding part of the MTN Whale Route), the gourmet (crayfish, or rocklobster, is a delicious speciality of the region) and the lover of sunshine, silence and tranquility.

THE COASTAL ROUTE

The road north from Cape Town, the R27, leads along the western seaboard past the grand dunefields around Atlantis and Yzerfontein, past Langebaan and Saldanha to Velddrif and beyond, to the atmospheric little fishing centre of Lambert's Bay. The land becomes drier, bleaker, the farther up the coast you travel but after the winter rains, when the warm breezes begin to blow and the pollinators are abroad, even the dreariest parts take on glorious colour. More often than not the best time to make the journey is at the end of August. The papery magenta beauty of sea lavender decorates the dunes and sandy stretches; Livingstone daisies bring dazzling colour to the roadsides; beyond are carpets of wild cinerarias, large white petalled daisies and much else. Farther north, around Lambert's Bay, the more arid countryside yields succulent-leafed vygies; creeping along the sand are yellow and orange helderkruipvygie (*Jordaaniella dubia*). Inland, the sandveld fynbos is also bright with annuals.

Daisies are among the wild flowers that decorate the Postberg section of the West Coast National Park. The area is open to visitors only in spring and early summer (August to October); animals to be seen include springbok, bontebok and black wildebeest.

By midsummer, the sun-bleached but striking red flowers of succulents – hondeoor, rooi suikerblom, *Aloe mitriformis* – appear in the more sheltered sandy and rocky areas. The amaryllids, some of which dry out to become the tumbleweeds one sees rolling before the wind, make a spectacular show in autumn.

If you're not especially pressed for time, consider starting your springtime excursion in the north, making your way slowly southwards as the flower season matures.

THE DARLING HILLS

Just inland from the ocean, about 80 km from Cape Town, is the little town of Darling, set among vineyards and golden wheatfields and hills whose slopes, in winter, host scatters of creamy white arum lilies. Here, the wild flowers of spring put on an exquisite show, no more so than in the Tienie Versfeld reserve. This 22-ha area protects a fragment of granitic soil that nurtures a host of species, most striking of which are bulb-like plants such as the multi-hued babianas and lachenalias; white, yellow, red and purple sundews (some of which are parasites; others carnivorous, feeding on insects); the 'evening flowers', or aandblomme, which scent the air at dusk, and the lovely chincherinchees, creamy blooms that are grown commercially in the area.

Flower-viewing visitors also enjoy easy access to a number of local farms, including Oudepost (which offers orchids), Contreberg, on the Darling-Mamre road (vlei flora), and Waylands, 6 km east of town (also vlei flora). A very special event is the Darling Wildflower Show, held during the third week of September, a time when some 300 different species are usually in full bloom. The Duckitt Orchid Show (exotic species) runs concurrently. Other features of local interest are the basket factory (hand-crafted ware) and the Butter Museum, an unusual show-case which emphasises just how significant a part the dairy industry plays in the region's economy.

THE WEST COAST NATIONAL PARK

Langebaan Lagoon, to the north of Darling, is a 16-km stretch of shallow, limpid water that probes down the coastal strip as an arm of Saldanha Bay.

Right: *The flower-bedecked shores of Langebaan Lagoon, focal point of the West Coast National Park. The waters, the sand- and mud-banks and the islands of nearby Saldanha Bay are a magnet for waders and seabirds.*

The lagoon is one of southern Africa's ornithological wonders: each year great flocks of migrant waders leave their Arctic breeding grounds, making their arduous, 20 000-km trans-Africa flight south to take up summer residence on and around its nutrient-rich waters, marshes and mudbanks. Even more prolific in bird life is the bay itself, its rugged shores and rocky little islands. The latter, isolated and free of predators, provide secure nesting sights for upwards of 670 000 cormorants, gannets, gulls, penguins and other seabirds.

Langebaan forms the centrepiece of the West Coast National Park, a spacious expanse of sandy terrain that sustains what, for most of the year, is a visually rather dull mix of dwarf bushes, sedges, succulents and fynbos (enlivened at times by bietou and *Limonium perigrinum*, known as strandroos).

Ixia curta Family Iridaceae. A perennial bulb-like plant (here seen with a visiting monkey beetle) that grows to some 15–40 cm tall. Found on sandy flats in the Darling and Malmesbury areas, it bears orange flowers with a brown to green centre during October.

Drosera cistiflora, sundew. Family Droseraceae. A low perennial, 10–40 cm tall, with sticky leaves adapted to capture insects. Grows on sandy flats and slopes near Clanwilliam, into Namaqualand and east to Port Elizabeth. The flowers, ranging from mauve to red, yellow and white, appear in early spring (August–September).

Spiloxene canaliculata. Family Hypoxidaceae. A bulb-like, low plantlet growing to 10–35 cm tall. Found on wet flats near Malmesbury and probably farther afield. Its flowers are produced in July–November.

Ornithogalum thyrsoides, chincherinchee, here visited by a 'heady maiden' moth. Family Hyacinthaceae. A bulb found on flats and lower slopes, often in vleis. Occurs from Gifberg to the Cape Peninsula, and north into Namaqualand. White flowers appear October–December.

In the spring season, though, the countryside is clothed in an extravagance of colour. The floral displays are usually at their most striking in the park's Postberg section, an 1 800-ha area of coastal plain and granite outcrop that also offers wildlife (springbok and other antelope), picnic spots and 25 km of game- and flower-viewing roads. Postberg is open only from August to October. The wider area can be explored, at any time of the year, on one or other of the conducted, 13- to 16-km educational trails.

The lagoon is a popular recreation area, most visitors overnighting in Langebaan village or at nearby Club Mykonos, a large and imaginatively conceived resort complex designed in traditional Aegean style.

THE SALDANHA AREA

Saldanha Bay is a fine natural harbour that was bypassed by the early European seafarers for lack of fresh water but has now been dredged and developed to accommodate some the largest of bulk carrier (principally iron-ore) vessels. The local economy recently received further impetus with the establishment of a huge steelworks and its satellite industries – none of which, it is claimed, will impact too severely on the sandveld and wetland environment. The area is also headquarters of the West Coast's fishing fleet.

For the rest, the bay is popular among yachtsmen, anglers, watersports enthusiasts, bird-watchers and the quieter, more relaxed kind of holidaymaker. The surrounding strandveld sustains much the same flora as the West Coast National Park (see above) but without the richness of the latter's Postberg section. A pleasant drive to the east will take you through countryside garlanded by Saldanha pincushions to the village of Hopefield, whose Fynbos Park is worth a brief visit.

Right: *A general store at the tiny West Coast village of Paternoster, home to hardy fishermen. Well worth viewing are the springtime wild flowers of close-by Columbine Nature Reserve.*

Calendar

SPRING; coastal: Lovely annuals grow between strandveld shrubs and sandveld fynbos, among them Livingstone daisies in dazzling variety along roadsides; drumsticks (*Zaluzianskya villosa*); leeubekkies (*Nemesia*); horinkies (*Diascia*) wild cineraria; some bulb-like plants. Shrubs are also attractive: daisy bushes, scrophs, green snake-stem pincushions and others.
Inland: plenty on display; Olifants River valley has showy annual daisies; perdeblom in rocky areas; Biedouw valley is a must for annuals and vygies, but check with Flowerline first (see below); spring comes later in the cooler mountains;

For up-to-date information, call the MTN Flowerline 083 910 1028 (June to October).

the yellow Clanwilliam daisy is seen between that town and Citrusdal; vygie flowers predominate north of Clanwilliam.

SUMMER; coastal: Not the best season, though the veld is brightened by the pink papery flowers of strandroos and, on granite outcrops, the scarlet flowerheads of hondeoor and rooisuikerblom.
Inland: a harsh time for flowers, though the Porterville area offers disas and ericas in January and February; mountain slopes may be carpeted in, among others, the bright pink of *Erica inflata*.

AUTUMN: Strandveld and sandveld fynbos generally dried out, but you'll see some spectacular amaryllids such as the large creamy, or pink, trumpet-shaped malgaslelie and powderbush. Not much inland.

WINTER; coastal: Brilliant blooms of early vygies in the drier north.
Inland: Mountain fynbos – proteas such as grey-leaf sugarbush.

Spring comes to St Helena Bay

To the north is the inland town of Vredenburg and, on the coast, the charming little fishing hamlets of Stompneusbaai and Paternoster, the latter named for the Latin prayer offered up by grateful survivors of an early shipwreck. Nearby Columbine Nature Reserve is noted for the beauty and profusion of its spring flowers; Velddrif, at the Berg River estuary, attracts great numbers of waterbirds, most notably flamingos, spoonbills and avocets. The Berg discharges into the broad, 20-km sweep of St Helena Bay, where Portuguese navigator Vasco da Gama made his landfall (in 1497). Today, fishing settlements and processing factories intrude on an otherwise pleasant shoreline scene, but stretching inland from the beaches are green pastures and fields of wheat – and, in September, a yellow, orange and white fantasia of wild flowers.

Above: *Looking across to Saldanha Bay, with the distinctive Adam and Eve rocks in the foreground.*
Opposite page: *Flower-bedecked marshy terrain, or vleiland, near Malmesbury.*
Below: *Cape gannets gather in their thousands on Bird island, Lambert's Bay.*

LAMBERTS BAY AND BEYOND

The coastal route north from Velddrif leads you, through increasingly dry terrain, to bird-rich Rocher Pan (where you'll see carpets of estuarine plants) and Elands Bay, at the mouth of Verlorenvlei – a splendid wetland haven for great numbers of waders and waterfowl, and for spring annuals. Here you'll find tolbos or the grey conebush (*Leucadendron pubescens*); leucadendrons, restios, gousblomme, senecio and, in the drier areas, colourful vygies decorate the land to the north.

Lamberts Bay, 48 km farther on, is an attractive little maritime centre whose harbour is invariably busy and bright with the movement and colours of its workworn fishing boats. It is also a bird-watcher's delight: joined to the harbour wall is an 'island' inhabited by a vast, closely packed and animated throng of gannets, Cape cormorants (in winter), seagulls and 'sterretjies'. Also in residence are a few jackass penguins and the occasional pelican. Lamberts Bay has an excellent hotel, and a wonderfully informal, open-air seafood eatery (see box; page 26). Cray-fishing trips are laid on for visitors.

The northward route leads on to the little seaside hamlets of Doring Bay, Strandfontein and Papendorp, at the estuary of the Olifants River. Sandstone cliffs between Doring Bay and Strandfontein hint of what Namaqualand has to offer in flower terms, harbouring charming miniature gardens of crassulas, conophytums and vygies. Roads turn inland (the R27 at Doring Bay; the R362 at Papendorp) to take you through superb wildflower countryside to the larger centres of Vredendal and Lutzville, both girded around by the green abundance of the river's valley. These towns also serve as attractive bases for exploring the wider area and its floral wealth.

THE INLAND ROUTE

The main highway north from Cape Town (the N7) leads you through the fertile Swartland region to the pleasant little towns of Citrusdal and Clanwilliam on the banks of the Olifants River. Here the countryside is fairly intensively farmed, but there are wild flowers aplenty to be seen and enjoyed in their season.

MALMESBURY TO PIKETBERG

These two small centres lie at the heart of the Swartland ('black country'), so named perhaps for the richness of its soils (which in fact are reddish-brown) and famed for its harvests of golden wheat, and for vineyards that produce some fine wines.

Malmesbury, a 45-minute drive from Cape Town, is among the oldest of South Africa's country settlements, founded in the valley of the Diep River in 1743 and once known for its curative springs. The first church to be built in the area, the Oude Kerk, now serves as a museum; in the nearby Riebeeck Valley stands the house in which Jan Christiaan Smuts, soldier and statesman, was born (it has been beautifully restored; visitors are welcome). Looming over the village of Riebeeck Kasteel, just to the northeast, is the 'castle mountain', where a nature walk leads visitors through an especially attractive fynbos area. In springtime, moreover, the hillsides – indeed the whole of the Riebeeck Valley – are exquisitely garlanded in the soft pinks and whites of peach blossom. On the farm Spes Bona is the country's biggest oak tree and, rather unusually, a museum devoted to wagon-making.

Moorreesburg, 40 km farther along the N7, is distinguished by its wheat museum, one of only three such in the world; Piketberg, the next town, by its lofty sandstone mountain, which hosted a colonial outpost or 'piquet' during the 17th-century hostilities between Dutch settlers and indigenous Khoikhoi.

CITRUSDAL AND CLANWILLIAM

The valley of the Olifants River is remarkably productive: rainfall is modest enough but there is generous run-off from the mountains to the east and the river's waters, captured and diverted by a well-engineered system of canals, nurtures fine crops of wine grapes, vegetables and, most especially, the orchards of Valencia oranges, grapefruit, lemons and easy-to-peel hybrids. For much of the year the air is heady with the scent of the fruit (see box). The area's natural vegetation is a form of fynbos especially attractive are the showy annuals and, in late spring, *Heliophila*, numerous skilpadbos species and grey conebush – and, in the northern parts, a smatter of succulent karoo species.

Citrusdal is the main centre of the citrus groves, the country's third most extensive but, because the winters are wet and frost free and summers are blessed by up to ten

ANCIENT ORCHARDS

Close to 100 000 tons of citrus fruit are harvested in the Citrusdal-Clanwilliam area between March and September. The groves are the country's third largest after those of the Sundays River valley in the Eastern Cape and the Northern Province's giant Zebediela estates. They are also by far the oldest: the first orchard was laid out in the 1660s, with seedlings from Jan van Riebeeck's Boskloof poperty in what is today's Claremont area of Cape Town, and over the centuries their progeny has flourished. Some of the trees are ancient; one especially venerable specimen, on the farm Groot Hexrivier, began bearing fruit a full 250 years ago and, remarkably, is still yielding its seasonal bounty.

Above: *The glory of the Clanwilliam Wildflower Garden.*
Below: *Fat oranges on display at a Citrusdal farmstall.*

hours of sunshine a day, they are arguably the finest in terms of product quality. The local Goede Hoop co-operative lays on in-season tours of its huge packing house in town. Just as well endowed is the countryside around Clanwilliam, some 30 km distant: orchards, vineyards and fields of wheat and emerald lucerne flourish under its hot sun. The area, though, is especially noted for its fragrant and reputedly curative rooibos 'tea', made from the sharp-leafed shrub *Aspalathus linearis* that grows wild (and is now cultivated) on the slopes of the Cederberg to the east. Features of note in Clanwilliam itself include the local drostdy, or magistrate's court (built in 1808), the elegant Dutch Reformed church (1864) and the Anglican church. This last is one of the more than 50 places of worship designed by the extraordinarily energetic and talented Sophy Gray, wife of Cape Town's first Anglican bishop (1848–72).

The wild flowers are perhaps seen at their most varied in the 54-ha Ramskop Nature Reserve. This lies at the northeastern corner of the Clanwilliam dam and in the rich transitional zone between the fynbos and the southern limits of the succulent karoo. It is criss-crossed by footpaths, one of them bringing you, circuitously, to a high point that commands memorable views – of the placid blue waters of the dam (ranked among the country's best for water-skiing), of the Olifants River running away to the northwest, and of the Cederberg's majesty to the east. A small (7.5-ha) cultivated part of the reserve, the Clanwilliam Wildflower Garden, is attractive home to more than 200 different flowering plant species.

Among the most rewarding of excursions from Clanwilliam is that which takes you eastwards, over the rocky Pakhuis Pass and down into the Biedouw valley, renowned for its quite stunning springtime floral displays. The season is very short; August is usually the best month, but just one or two berg winds can wilt the flowers, so do check with the MTN Flowerline (see page 5) before setting out. A digression southward will bring you to the enchanting little village of Wuppertal, which started life, in 1830, as a Rhenish mission station and has changed little over the decades since (though the place now boasts a restaurant, and limited facilities for overnight visitors).

Above: *Fine examples of Bushman (or San) rock art decorate the Stadshal cave complex in the Cederberg mountains.*
Below: *The Wolfberg Arch is among the most prominent of the Cederberg's many unusual rock formations.*

THE CEDERBERG

For sheer visual drama, few parts of the Western Cape can compare with the Cederberg, the ruggedly rocky, 100-km long range of mountains than rises splendidly above the vineyards and citrus groves of the Olifants River valley.

Most of the uplands lie within a controlled wilderness area, a 71 000-ha expanse of soaring peaks (the Sneeuberg, at 2 028 m above sea level, is the highest) and plunging ravines, of clear streams and waterfalls, caves, cliffs and overhangs, and rock formations that have been weathered by wind and water into a remarkable fantasia of stark and often strange shapes.

The mountains are home to a modest variety of animals, including baboon, caracal, the pretty little bat-eared fox and a number of elusive antelope species, and to a surprisingly prolific bird life (the raptors are rather special), but are best known for the superb diversity of endemic mountain fynbos. One of the rarest of the flowering plants is the pure-white snow protea or sneeublom *Protea cryophila*, which grows above the snowline and bares its large, low-growing flower-head in summer. Other plants,

Amaryllis belladonna, March Lily. Family Amaryllidaceae. A bulb, up to 90 cm tall, with several channelled leaves which appear after flowering. Grows on lower slopes in the Olifants valley to Peninsula and east to George; especially profuse after fire. The flowers, large bells in shades of pink, appear February–April.

Watsonia marginata, kanolpypie. Family Iridaceae. A bulb-like plant, up to 1.6 m tall, with broad leaves and pink flowers but also has dwarf white to purple forms. It grows in sandy soils around Nieuwoudtville and farther south and east, to the Peninsula and Worcester. Flowers September–November.

Erica thunbergii, Malay heath. Family Ericaceae. A delicate plant reaching a height of 60 cm. It grows at high altitudes (about 1 100 m) in the Cederberg and Ceres areas. The flowers, which dazzle with their red and yellow combination, appear September–November.

Aloe comosa. Family Asphodelaceae. A single stem growing up to 2 m in height, found on the dry slopes around Clanwilliam and also Botterkloof. The attractive ivory-pink flowers appear in summer (December–January).

Albuca clanwilliamae-gloria. Family Hyacinthaceae. This bulb, a tall plant growing to 1.5–2 m, is found in sandy soils among restios in the fynbos, and endemic to the region between the towns of Klawer and Clanwilliam. It produces its flowers in spring.

Babiana scabrifolia, bobbejaantjie. Family Iridaceae. A bulb-like plant with low foliage, 3–9 cm tall, found on sandy soils in the Clanwilliam area. The flowers, blue but ranging to lilac and with yellow and purple markings, are produced in June–August.

FLORAL HIGHLIGHTS: THE CEDERBERG

Paranomus bracteolaris, smooth-leaf tree sceptre. Family Proteaceae. The pink parts of this shrub's flowerhead are just visible beneath a thick white woolly growth. Grows on sandstone sands at mid slopes. Flowers August–October.

Erica tumida. Family Ericaceae. Shrubs may reach up to 1.6 m in height. Grows at 700–1900 m altitude on mountain ranges from from Clanwilliam to Worcester. The plant produces spectacular shows – the entire bush covered in slightly swollen tubular flowers of bright red – from October to February.

Leucospermum catherinae, Catherine-wheel pincushion. Family Proteaceae. A tall shrub with pale orange flower parts. They are found alone, occasionally in large stands, on sandstone soils along streamsides from Cederberg to Koue Bokkeveld, also Piketberg. Flowers appear September–December.

Leucadendron procerum, ivory conebush. Family Proteaceae. A 3 m-tall shrub whose outer bracts are pale green to ivory; inner cone-like cluster of male florets are red. Grows in dense stands on sandstone sands. Flowers appear in August.

the babianas and showy springtime pelargoniums, the gladiola and pincushions, grace the slopes in greater profusion to fashion, in their season, a quite entrancing floral tapestry.

The Cederberg also supports some handsome indigenous trees. Indeed the range takes its name from the stately Clanwilliam cedar *Widdringtonia cedarbergensis*, which once flourished in the uplands but was brought to the edge of extinction, in the early colonial days, by climate change, uncontrolled burning and the settlers' greed for timber. A few specimens survived in the higher parts and, now strictly protected, will hopefully provide the nucleus for future generations.

The mountains are a magnet for hikers, campers, climbers and lovers of nature at its grandest. Main access is via the road east from a point 30 km beyond Citrusdal, which takes you over the Nieuwoudt Pass (fine views along the way) to the peaceful and most attractive Algeria forest station and camping ground.

A 250-km network of paths enables you to explore the wilderness area with relative ease, but do make sure you go out armed with a forestry map showing the routes. Longer-distance hikers can overnight in mountain huts.

The Maltese Cross rises sentinel-like above the rock-strewn upper slopes of the Cederberg.

FLORAL HIGHLIGHTS: THE WEST COAST

Carpobrotus acinaciformis, sour fig. Family Mesembryanthemaceae. A sprawling shrublet with thick succulent leaves distinctly scimitar-like in shape. Found mainly on sandy soils from Malmesbury to Peninsula and Hermanus. The brilliant magenta flowers appear August–October.

Dimorphotheca pluvialis, reën-blommetjie. Family Asteraceae. An annual plant, 10–40 cm tall, which is widespread on slopes and flats along the West Coast, north to Namaqualand and Namibia, south to Peninsula, and east to Riversdale. Flowers, white with purple reverse, appear August–October.

Dorotheanthus bellidiformis, Livingstone daisy, bokbaaivygie. Family Mesembryanthemaceae. These annual herbs have glistening leaves and bright white, pink, yellow, red or purple flowers. Mostly a coastal species but also found inland (north and east to Bredasdorp). Flowers appear August–September.

Massonia angustifolia, bobbe-jaanboek. Family Hyacinthaceae. A bulb with broad succulent leaves pressed to the ground like an open book. Flowers are white, yellow or red in a dense cluster between the leaves. Found around Saldanha, and also into Namaqualand and Karoo. Flowers May–June.

Lachenalia aloides, Cape cowslip, vierkleurtjie. Family Hyacinthaceae. An 8–15 cm tall bulb with flowers that are red and yellow with green tips. Grows around Citrusdal, Piketberg and south to Cape Peninsula. Flowers apear July–October.

Moraea villosa ssp. ***villosa,*** peacock moraea. Family Iridaceae. A bulb-like plant, 40 cm tall, with hairy leaves and flowers that are purple, blue, white or orange. Grows on stony ground on slopes and flats around Citrusdal, and from Piketberg to Gordon's Bay. Flowers August–September.

Lachenalia viridiflora. Family Hyacinthaceae. This bulb, 8–10 cm tall, has green flowers that are produced June–July. It grows on granite hills and is endemic to the Vredenburg area.

Spiloxene capensis, sterretjie. Family Hypoxidaceae. A bulb-like plantlet, growing 10–30 cm tall, found from Clanwilliam to Tulbagh and Cape Peninsula, east to Port Elizabeth. The flowers, yellow or white and sometimes iridescent in the middle, appear August–November.

FLORAL HIGHLIGHTS: THE WEST COAST

Babiana ringens, rotstert. Family Iridaceae. A bulb-like plant, 15–40 cm tall, with bright red flowers borne on a side branch; main axis lacks flowers and resembles an upright rat's tail. It grows on sandy flats and lower slopes from Clanwilliam to Peninsula and to Bredasdorp. Flowers August–October.

Leucospermum tomentosum, Saldanha pincushion. Family Proteaceae. A shrub with flower-heads about 3.5 cm in diameter. Listed in Red Data Book as vulnerable; limited distribution on sand flats near the sea around Hopefield and Vredenburg to Bokbaai. Flowers June–November.

Zaluzianskya villosa, drumsticks. Family Scrophulariaceae. A low hairy annual, 6–30 cm tall, whose white or mauve flowers tend to remain closed during the day, opening at dusk to synchronize with its pollinators. Grows Nieuwoudtville to Caledon and north to Namaqualand; also in Karoo. Flowers June–November.

Leucospermum hypophyllocarpo-dendron, green snake-stem pincushion. Family Proteaceae. A trailing plant about 20 cm tall, spreading over 1.5 m, with upright leaves. Grows on low-lying sandy flats from the Berg River valley to the Peninsula (now extinct on the Cape Flats) and on the Elim coastal flats. Flowers in spring.

Zantedeschia aethiopica, arum lily. Family Araceae. A perennial, up to 1 m tall, with white flowers. It grows in damp places, and is found throughout the Western Cape and north as far as Mpumalanga. Cultivated world wide. Flowers June–October.

Nemesia versicolor, leeubekkie. Family Scrophulariaceae. An annual that grows to 10–50 cm in height. Found on sandy flats from Clanwilliam to Knysna and in Namaqualand. The flowers, often with striped reverse, appear August–November.

Gethyllis afra, kukumakranka. Family Amaryllidaceae. A bulb with twisted spiral leaves. The flowers are white with red band on reverse; fruits are a skinny banana shape. Grows on flats but occurs rather rarely; found from Clanwilliam to Peninsula to Caledon. Flowers in summer.

Agathosma thymifolia, buchu. Family Rutaceae. A shrub that grows up to 1 m in height, highly branched, with clusters of mauve flowers. Found on coastal sand on limestone. Endemic to the area around Saldanha and Yzerfontein. Flowers appear August–October.

The Cape Metropolitan Area

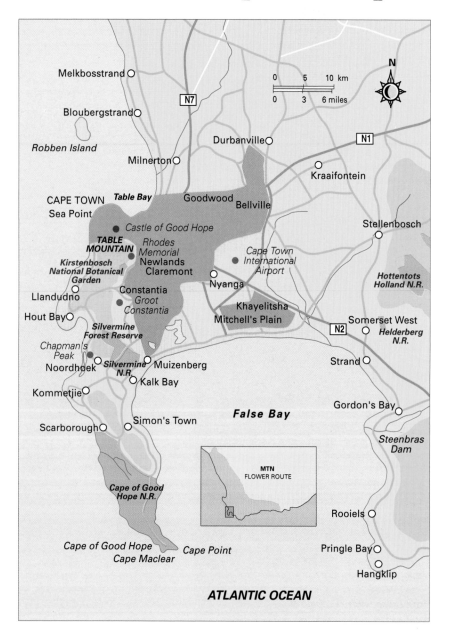

*F*ew cities can claim so magnificent a setting as Cape Town: its central district huddles beneath the moody majesty of Table Mountain, one of the best-known of the world's natural landmarks, its suburbs stretching across the flatlands to the north and east, and southwards down the narrow, 75-km long, hook-shaped finger of land known as the Cape Peninsula. The latter comprises, for the most part, a 'spine' of imposing and quite beautiful mountains and hills that end, dramatically, at the massive headland of Cape Point.

Within the wider Cape Metropolitan Area, which ranges from damp green mountain slopes to windswept sandy plains, thrive the plants that make up one of the six and by far the smallest of the world's floral kingdoms. Altogether, the Cape Floral Kingdom encompasses some 8 500 species, of which more than 2 250 are found on the Peninsula itself.

Indeed, the Peninsula has arguably the world's highest concentration of plant species. About 200 are endemic – found growing naturally nowhere else. This extraordinary diversity is due in part to the huge variation in soil type and climate: rainfall, for example, averages 300 mm a year at Cape Point, while the suburb of Newlands, not too far away, enjoys more than 2 000 mm.

The area sustains a number of different vegetation types, most notably fynbos – hardy, small-leaved shrubs which grow in poor soils and are subject to periodic fires. Its characteristic plant forms are the proteas (such as those in Family Proteaceae); heath-like ericas (Family Ericaceae for example); reedy restioids (Restionaceae) and bulb-like species. Mountain fynbos is found in the higher, rockier parts of the Peninsula.

Sand plain fynbos – a type that grows, obviously, on sandy plains – has been largely destroyed by urban development, surviving only in the Noordhoek basin and towards Cape Point in the south. Similarly, tiny pockets of dune fynbos and thicket, including small stands of milkwood trees, can still be seen at Noordhoek, Kommetjie and Gifkommetjie in the Cape of Good Hope section of the Cape Peninsula National Park.

Patches of indigenous forest flourish in Newlands and Kirstenbosch in the southern suburbs, in the mountains above Noordhoek; and in the Orange Kloof area along the upper sections of the Hout Bay valley. Orange Kloof sustains such trees as Cape beech, yellowwood, wild olive, assegai , rooi-els, and a huge wild peach tree reputed to be the largest specimen in existence. The kloof and its surrounds are good walking country, especially in January and February when visitors can see the lovely *Disa uniflora*, also known as the pride of Table Mountain. Orchids also thrive. Bulbs are spectacular in spring or just after a scheduled burn.

Small areas of renosterveld – dull, shrubby plants dominated by the renosterbos (*Elytropappus rhinocerotis*) and enlivened by spectacular bulbs in spring and autumn – are found on shale soils on Devil's Peak, Lion's Head and at Llandudno. The renosterveld on the eastern slopes of Devil's Peak and Table Mountain has been replaced by grasslands grazed by wildebeest, eland, zebra and bontebok.

Much of the wider area's indigenous flora is at risk: human encroachment and the proliferation of alien plants have taken their toll, and it is reckoned that more than 1 000 species are now threatened with extinction (though not all have been formally classified as such). The future, however, holds some promise: in 1998 large parts of the Peninsula were proclaimed as the Cape Peninsula National Park, a status that should go a long way towards preserving the region's precious natural heritage.

TABLE MOUNTAIN

The sandstone mountain rises more than a thousand metres above the city and Table Bay, its straight-edged summit stretching three kilometres from end to end. On either side, guarding its flanks like gigantic sentinels, are Lion's Head and Devil's Peak – formations that are almost as distinctive in shape and character as the mountain itself. To the west, lining the Atlantic seaboard and forming an integral part of the Table Mountain range, is a 15–km long series of rugged, often mist-wreathed heights known as the Twelve Apostles.

The mountain's table-top is quite narrow, plunging away to the back plateau – a magical place of footpaths and flowers. Indeed, more than half the Cape Peninsula's 2 000-plus fynbos species and most of its indigenous trees are to be found on the slopes. The shimmering silver tree *Leucadendron argenteum*, one of the largest of the protea family (see box on this page), is found on the moister east-facing slopes running from Devil's Peak south to Newlands.

Among the mountain's numerous other notable species are the waboom or wagon tree (*Protea nitida*) with its large, attractively creamy flowerheads; stretches of restio or Cape reed on the front of the mountain table; the creamy, red-tipped bracts of the endemic male and female Peninsula conebush plant (*Leucadendron strobilinum*) on the higher levels; and the emerald-headed green sugarbush (*Protea coronata*).

THE TREE THAT SHIMMERS
Among the tallest of the protea family is the silver tree *Leucadendron argenteum*, which can grow to more than 15 metres high (though it averages much less). Its name alludes to the silky, silvery hairs covering the pale green leaves. The tree is at its most attractive when the leaves shimmer in the strong winds that sweep the Cape.

It is said that the silver tree will flourish only within sight of Table Mountain, but specimens are to be found in the Cape winelands and it has been successfully cultivated much farther afield. The species is fairly easy to grow, though it seems to be prone to fungal infection and tends to die suddenly and without warning.

On the drier western slopes, above the beaches of Camps Bay and Oudekraal, are dense stands of vaalkreupelhout (*Leucospermum conocarpodendron*). From June to September the deep-pink flowers of the endemic *Erica conica* appear on the back of Table Mountain and the north-eastern slopes of the nearby Constantiaberg. Growing in damp sites near Maclear's Beacon (the Peninsula's highest point) are pink, urn-shaped flowers of *Erica pilulifera*, a species endemic to the Peninsula mountains.

For walkers and climbers, there are hundreds of charted routes along and up the slopes, some of them undemanding, many arduous, a few downright dangerous unless one is an experienced mountaineer. Anyone intending to explore the mountain on foot should make careful preparations for the excursion: arm yourself with a good map, water, sunblock and warm clothing (sudden mists can descend, even in summer). And stick to the paths.

Most visitors, however, take the cable car to the top, a quick and comfortable ride. The car rotates, providing passengers with a variety of fine vistas; at the summit there are pleasant restaurants, gift shop (from which faxes and postcards, bearing the Table Mountain postmark, can be sent), wall-plaques that describe the mountain's flora in all their seasons, pathways that lead away from the cable station, and observation sites. The

Top: *A scene on the summit of Table Mountain showing typical ground cover.*
Above: *Looking towards the upper cable station; the flowers in the foreground are grey tree pincushions in their full spring glory.*
Above right: *Panoramic vistas unfold from the cable-car; the trip to the top of the mountain takes about four minutes.*
Right: *The mountain and its cable station viewed from Lion's Head, with* Pelargonium cucullatum *in the foreground.*

CITY HIGHLIGHTS

Victoria & Alfred Waterfront: The city's premier eating, drinking, entertainment, specialist-shopping venue. Hotels, museums, marina, world-class Two Oceans Aquarium, restaurants for all tastes, bistros, brewery, wine centre, theatre, giant-screen Imax cinema, craft and produce markets, excursions by boat (to Robben Island among other destinations) and helicopter.

Castle of Good Hope: Massive five-sided fortress, completed 1679; period furnishings; art gallery (Flemish masterpieces); temporary art and craft displays; innovative theatre/cabaret; guided tours.

Adderley Street: The central business district shopping thoroughfare; fresh-flower market; Groote Kerk (Dutch Reformed mother church).

Old Slave Lodge Top of Adderley Street; now a museum of fascinating exhibits drawn from different cultures, including European and Chinese, though emphasis remains on South Africa's heritage.

Bo-Kaap: Old Malay Quarter: Historic home to part of city's Islamic community, many members of whom are descended from slaves; charming 18th-century flat-roofed houses; narrow streets, mosques, museum.

Greenmarket Square: Cobbled piazza; home to the city's liveliest market; notable buildings include imposing Methodist Church and Old Town House (art gallery).

Company Garden, just south of the city centre: originally (1652) a vegetable garden planted by the first Dutch settlers, now a pleasant place for strolling; numerous exotic trees, shrubs and flowering plants; aviary; orchids and palms in conservatory; open-air restaurant. The area is flanked by some fine buildings (Parliament and National Gallery).

South African Museum, Victoria Street: San (Bushman) culture; Karoo fossils; geological, archaeological, natural history specimens; whale well and much else. Planetarium next door.

---

views are spectacular, though the heights are often mantled in billowing clouds that plunge, like a tumultuous waterfall, down the mountain's precipitous north face. This phenomenon, a product of the strong Cape south-easter wind, is a source of endless fascination to watchers in the city streets far below.

KIRSTENBOSCH NATIONAL BOTANICAL GARDEN

This splendid, 530-ha, wind-protected expanse of land on the steep, well-watered eastern slopes of the Table Mountain range offers a concentrated insight into the country's immense floral wealth – and thus serves as an ideal introduction for visitors intent on exploring the greater floral kingdom.

Around 6 000 species of indigenous plants are to be seen and enjoyed within the garden's relatively small cultivated area, among them a fine diversity of proteas, ericas, cycads, succulents, restios, mesembryanthemums and pelargoniums. These last are endemic to South Africa, but many have been hybridized to produce the geraniums that decorate garden beds and window boxes the world over.

An Egyptian goose navigates its way among pond-loving blue water-lilies at Kirstenbosch. The garden is world famous for the variety of its plants.

Agapanthus africanus. Family Amaryllidaceae; 30–50 cm tall; common on the upper slopes of the mountain chain; flowers December–March. An example of a genus which has become a popular garden subject elsewhere in the world.

Syncarpha vestita, everlasting or sewe-jaartjie. Asteraceae or daisy family. Afrikaans common name derives from the papery flowers, which are said to last seven years. Very common in the Cape of Good Hope reserve. Flowers November–January, usually some 2–5 years after a fire.

Aristea major, blousuurkanol. Family Iridaceae; up to 1.5 m tall; found on the Peninsula's lower mountain slopes but also more widely spread, occurring from Piketberg in the north to the Cape Peninsula, and west to Caledon. This specimen was photographed above the seaside suburb of Camps Bay. The blue blooms appear from October to December.

Disa uniflora, pride of Table Mountain. Family Orchidaceae; emblem of the Western Province, often found along mountain streams and in wet ravines. Flowers January–March. The plant belongs to the 'red guild' of summer blooms that are pollinated by just one species of brown butterfly.

Brachysiphon fucatus. Family Penaeaceae, which is endemic to the Cape. The shrublet is rare, found on the northern Peninsula mountains; grows in wet mountain fynbos. Flowers appear from May to September.

Nerine sarniensis, Guernsey lily. Family Amaryllidaceae. Flowers March–May; leaves are produced only later and are strap-shaped.

Erica abietina var. *echiiflora*, Family Ericaceae. This variety is confined to the saddle between Devil's Peak and the base of the upper section of Table Mountain. It grows in damp sites and flowers from August to September.

Gladiolus carneus, painted lady. Family Iridaceae. Found from the Cape Peninsula to the Outeniqua mountains, best displays seen along streams after fire. The pink blooms with their red markings attract long-tongued flies which pollinate the long tubular flowers. Flowers October to mid-November.

Cyrtanthus ventricosus, fire lily. Family Amaryllidaceae. Grows from Cape Peninsula to Mossel Bay. Bright red pendulous flowers from December–May.

Protea speciosa, brown-bearded sugarbush. Family Proteaceae. Grows on cool south slopes from the Peninsula through the Hottentots Holland range to the Langeberg. Flowers June–January but mainly September–October.

Leucospermum conocarpodendron, grey tree pincushion, also known as vaalkreupelhout. Family Proteaceae. A tree-like pincushion with a single stout trunk, endemic to the Peninsula; found from Devil's Peak to Llandudno on dry north and west slopes. Flowers August–December.

Watsonia tabularis. Family Iridaceae. Endemic to the Peninsula, and named after Table Mountain; frequently seen in marshy places from Constantiaberg to Kalk Bay. Found from sea level to 1 000 m. Typical form has salmon flowers in November–February. Pollinated by lesser double-collared sunbird.

Brabejum stellatifolium, wild almond. Family Proteaceae. Has only two florets per bract, and these are borne on long spikes. Grows from Gifberg to the Peninsula and to the Langeberg. Bears large velvety almond-shaped fruits. Flowers from December–January.

Leucadendron strobilinum, Peninsula conebush. Family Proteaceae. A Table Mountain endemic, found on damp, rocky south slopes, mainly from Table Mountain to Constantiaberg. Flowers September–October.

Roella ciliata. Family Campanulaceae. Either a scrambling or erect shrublet, frequently seen on the Cape Peninsula. Flowers from October to March.

Right: *The view from the grounds of Kirstenbosch towards the heights of Table Mountain. Some 6 000 different indigenous plant species are cultivated within the garden.*
Below right: *The lovely Tokai valley, seen from the northern slopes of the Silvermine reserve; the mountains to the left overlook the Constantia valley.*

ALIEN PLANTS

One of the biggest threats to the floral richness of the Cape Kingdom is the aggressive invasion of alien plants from other continents. Free of their usual limitations, such as pests and disease, they outgrow and stifle local species. Most aliens are large trees or shrubs, among them acacias, hakeas and pines. Not only do they threaten the local flora and animals with extinction but, because of their height, they burn with almost unquenchable ferocity. They also have an enormous thirst: compared to the moisture-thrifty fynbos, aliens draw excessive amounts of water from the ground and into the air. Happily, large-scale government-driven clearing programmes are underway, schemes that also teach skills and provide job opportunities.

Kirstenbosch's plants are grouped according to type, with sections devoted to fynbos; succulent plants; ancient cycads (which first appeared on earth about 150 million years ago) and many others. A network of neatly paved paths provides easy viewing, and conducted tours are laid on. The new Visitors' Centre, which has a large glass conservatory, features bulbs and succulents. For the visually impaired there is a fragrance garden and Braille route. The former offers plants with aromatic leaves or special textures, grown in waist-high beds; visitors on the latter follow a guide-rope for almost half a kilometre, stop-ping at points where the flora is described in large print and in Braille. A nearby display kiosk exhibits labelled examples of flowers currently to be seen in the grounds. There is also a herb garden. Part of the Dutch colonial leader Jan van Riebeeck's almond hedge (the wild almond is a member of the protea family) can still be seen. It was planted in the 1650s, and what remains of it is now a national monument.

The rest of Kirstenbosch, the larger part by far, remains in its natural state (though some exotics were introduced in earlier times). Beautifully forested, it is accessible via forest paths and the Camphor Walk, routes that take you up the hillside along avenues of fig, camphor, ironwood, yellowwood and other handsome trees. The bird life is a joy, especially in springtime.

Near what was the main the gate (the main entrance is now at the new Visitor's Centre at the bottom of the gardens), there is a pleasant restaurant serving breakfast, lunch and tea, and a nursery that stocks a fine array of plants. The Visitors' Centre has a coffee shop and lifestyle store that stocks books, clothes, aromatherapy oils, jewellery, crafts and tableware. Sunday concerts are held in the grounds on balmy summer evenings; the weekend craft market, opposite the main gates, is well worth a browse.

TOWARDS SILVERMINE

From the T-junction just to the south of Kirstenbosch, the road (Rhodes Drive) bears right and winds its way up the slopes to Constantia Nek – an enchanting woodland drive. To the right is Cecilia Forest, a place of tall, exotic trees, winding tracks and a lovely waterfall.

At Constantia Nek one has the choice of two routes, both scenically superb: to the west is the hill-girded coastal town and harbour of Hout Bay; to the east the beautifully embowered Constantia valley. The latter encompasses the vineyards of Groot Constantia, among the oldest and grandest of the country's Cape Dutch homesteads and one of three estates comprising the Constantia wine route. Groot Constantia offers wine tastings and sales, a wine museum, two restaurants and picnic spots in the most elegant of grounds. The manor-house itself is splendidly furnished in period style.

FOR BIRD-LOVERS
Rondevlei: This nature reserve, near Muizenberg on the east coast, is home to some 220 bird species. There are footpaths, a picnic area, observation points, hides; hippo in residence. Best months to visit: January to April.
Rietvlei, north of the city: This is the region's premier waterfowl breeding area; migrants from Europe arrive in late spring. It's also a centre for the rehabilitation of injured and polluted seabirds.
World of Birds, Hout Bay. The country's largest bird park contains 450 mainly exotic species (3 000-plus individuals altogether) in spacious, land-scaped walk-through aviaries.

Pelargonium cucullatum, wildemalva. Family Geraniaceae. Up to 2 m tall, a robust shrub which grows on coastal flats and lower slopes from the Peninsula to Bredasdorp and also at Saldanha on the West Coast. Flowers September–February.

Chasmanthe aethiopica, suurkanol. Family Iridaceae. 40–80 cm tall, occasional, grows under trees and in damp places on mountain slopes and plateaus; mainly coastal, from the Peninsula to Port Elizabeth. Flowers April–June.

Erica mammosa. Family Ericaceae. 50–100 cm tall, widespread, so flowers are variable in colour, ranging through dark red, greenish cream and shades of pink. Found from the Cederberg through the Peninsula and Stellenbosch to Caledon; from sea level to the higher slopes, but favours sandy seep.

Crassula coccinea, klipblom. Family Crassulaceae. Grows up to 50 cm tall, frequent on mountains (on rocky ledges) from Peninsula to Paarl and east to Bredasdorp. Scarlet blooms, flowers January–March. A member of the 'red guild' pollinated by one species of brown butterfly.

Ixia polystachya. Family Iridaceae. 30–38 cm tall, often found in damp sites, or in shade on flats and mountain slopes; locally common above Kirstenbosch. Flowers appear October–December.

Dilatris corymbosa, rooiwortel. Family Haemodoraceae. 40–60 cm tall, mauve blooms. Grows on slopes and flats from Tulbagh to Peninsula and east to Caledon. Flowers August–January.

Oxalis polyphylla, vingersuring. Family Oxalidaceae. 5–11 cm tall. Frequently grows on hill slopes from Ceres to Peninsula and east to Caledon and Port Elizabeth. The blooms are rose, lilac, or white. Flowers appear March–June.

Liparia splendens, mountain dahlia. Family Fabaceae. The shrub grows from 30 cm–2.5 m tall. Orange flowers in dense heads. An occasional on hill and mountain slopes, found from Paarl and the Peninsula to Mossel Bay. Flowers January–December.

Farther on is the turn-off to the M3 city highway. Follow the signs to Fish Hoek and Simon's Town via Ou Kaapse Weg (Old Cape Road) – an enchanting scenic drive over the high Steenberg range and then down into the flatlands of the Fish Hoek valley.

The terrain to either side of Ou Kaapse Weg is part of the Silvermine Nature Reserve, a magnificent, 2 000-ha upland expanse of fynbos countryside that runs above the narrow waist of the Peninsula. An intensive effort is underway to rid the area, now part of the Cape Peninsula National Park, of its invasive alien vegetation, restoring the land to the ericas, proteas, restios, spring flowering bulbs and other indigenous plants. Especially notable are the dense pockets of golden conebush; the common pagoda tree, whose striking coral bracts can be seen almost year-round; the blackbeard sugarbush, with its attractive cream to pink winter flowerheads; the lovely white and yellow *Erica lutea*, which blooms from February to May, and *Erica urna-viridis*, a Peninsula endemic named for the big, greenish bells which appear in late summer. Springtime brings carpets of orange-hued watsonias and the hanging bells of *Liparia splendens*. Silvermine is superb for walking. Picnic spots, viewsites and a number of routes, ranging from half an hour to half a day, have been established. Scatterings of purple *Pelargonium cucullatum* appear on the slopes above Kommetjie.

THE CAPE OF GOOD HOPE

One of the coastal region's largest expanses of protected fynbos countryside sprawls over the southern tip of the Peninsula, coming to a spectacular conclusion at its most prominent physical feature: the soaring cliffs of Cape Point. The 8 000-ha reserve is included in the Cape Peninsula park. There are panoramic views from the base of the old lighthouse, set atop massive cliffs that plunge 300 m to the blue ocean and reached either on foot (hard going) or by funicular. It is off the Point that the *Flying Dutchman*, the phantom ship of legend, has reputedly been sighted.

Alien vegetation, which despoiled parts of the area in the past, has now all but disappeared and much of the countryside is pristine, sustaining around 1 100 fynbos species. Springtime is glorious, though for much of the year the scenery has little immediate appeal; indeed in some months it is almost lunar in its starkness, its landscapes best viewed in the soft light of early morning or evening. The flowers tend to be small and go largely unnoticed unless sought out. The sandy areas sustain sand plain fynbos, among which is the thistle sugarbush (*Protea scolymocephala*) whose large, creamy, dish-like flowerheads flourish in late winter. Close to the coast you'll find wild rosemary (*Eriocephalus*), which has grey aromatic leaves and also

PENINSULA HIGHLIGHTS

Robben Island: In Table Bay, longtime prison to Nelson Mandela, now a moving monument to the liberation struggle; also a nature reserve, boat excursions leave from the Waterfront.

Rhodes Memorial: On eastern slopes of Table Mountain; neo-classical temple, powerful equestrian bronze, stone lions commemorate the controversial 19th-century tycoon, politician and visionary Cecil John Rhodes; tea garden; fine views.

Irma Stern Museum, Rosebank: Displays works of this talented and prolific South African artist in her original home; also houses changing exhibits by contemporary artists.

Wine route: Groot Constantia (below); Klein Constantia; Buitenverwachting, in the lovely Constantia Valley; all three welcome visitors.

Muizenberg: Superb beach; also Natale Labia museum (artworks) and Rhodes's cottage.

Simon's Town: Steeped in naval history; museums; nearby Boulders beachfront is home to a large colony of rare African (jackass) penguins.

Hout Bay: On western seaboard; attractive harbour; Mariner's Wharf complex; World of Birds (see box, page 43); boat trips to nearby Duiker Island and its lively colony of Cape fur seals.

Whale-watching: The Peninsula's coasts are on the MTN Whale Route; these giant marine mammals come close inshore in winter and spring.

ADAPTING TO FIRE

Fynbos has evolved to endure and even benefit from the autumn fires that often flare up after the hot, dry 'Mediterranean-climate' summers. Many plants are destroyed by fire and depend on their seeds for continued survival; others are protected by thick bark; still others are burnt to the ground and send up fresh growth. Some bulbs only flower after a fire when there is no competition for pollinators from the burnt surrounds. Many proteas hold their sealed cones on the mother plant to safeguard their seeds until the heat of an autumn fire unlocks the cones, whereafter the seeds are scattered on the ground in time for the first winter rains. Others time their seed output for summer, when ants are active. Tasty morsels attached to the seeds attract the ants, which carry the seeds below ground, safe from fire.

The Cape of Good Hope reserve, which occupies the Peninsula's southern tip, is home to more than 1 000 fynbos species. Many are small, insignificant plants, and for most of the year the countryside has little immediate appeal, but springtime brings a feast for the eyes.

produces its white flowers in late winter. Slightly inland are the low, fine-leafed shrubs of dune fynbos, dull for the most part but brightened in spring by the big purple flowers of birch-leafed pelargonium (*Pelargonium betulinum*). The extensive, central flats nurture fields of russet restioids and the bobbing, silvery heads of everlastings (*Syncarpha vestita* and *Edmondia sesamoides*). Ericas provide bright patches of colour in summer; late winter-flowering marsh pagoda (*Mimetes hirtus*), listed as vulnerable in the Red Data Book, grows abundantly in boggy areas; the route to Olifantsbos is through golden conebush (*Leucadendron laureolum*) shrubland. Just off the circular drive you'll see, in their season, the bizarre yellow and black flowers of *Witsenia maura*.

Roads and footpaths cut through the reserve. Facilities include a restaurant, shop, picnic sites and beach-bathing spots.

FLORAL HIGHLIGHTS: CAPE OF GOOD HOPE RESERVE

Mimetes hirtus, marsh pagoda. Family Proteaceae. A Peninsula endemic, now extinct from Rondebosch to Silvermine but dense stands are still found on marshes, seeps, streambanks in the Cape of Good Hope reserve and at Betty's Bay. Flowers from May–November, mainly in July and August.

Serruria villosa, golden spider-head. Family Proteaceae. A lowish shrub, 30–50 cm tall, flowerheads have yellowish, hairy parts and are strongly sweet-scented. Common, grows on south Peninsula only. Flowers appear April–July.

Berzelia lanuginosa, vleiknopbos. Family Bruniaceae. A member of a near-endemic Cape family. A much-branched shrub that grows 1.5–2 m tall. Found from the Cederberg to Worcester, the Peninsula and east to Bredas-dorp. Creamy flowerheads June–November.

Stilbe ericoides. Family Stilbaceae, endemic to the Cape Floral Kingdom. Either an erect or straggly shrub; 15–80 cm tall, with pinkish to mauve blooms. Grows on sandy flats or lime-stone hills from the Peninsula (frequent on dryish flats) to Swellendam and Uitenhage. Flowers May–September.

Haemanthus coccineus, April fool. Family Amaryllidaceae. 6–20 cm tall, scarlet flowers. Grows in coastal scrub and lower mountain slopes from Peninsula to Riversdale; also found as far as Namaqualand and Eastern Cape. Flowers in autumn, when plant has no leaves; latter appear later and are tongue-shaped.

Moraea ramosissima, geeltulp. Family Iridaceae. 50–90 cm tall, found from Gifberg to Peninsula, and east to Port Elizabeth. Locally common on the Peninsula, often in damp semi-shade in the northern areas. Stunning yellow blooms; flowers appear from October–December.

Oxalis luteola, suring. Family Oxalidaceae. 5–8 cm tall, dwarf plant, yellow flowers, leaves basal and hairy. Grows from Clanwilliam to Peninsula, and east to Riversdale. Flowers appear May–August.

Erica phylicifolia. Family Ericaceae. A robust plant with a sticky, reddish-purple, tubular flower. Common on the Peninsula, especially on moun-tain slopes of the southern parts, also on Hottentots Holland. Flowers September–June.

Protea lorea, thongleaf sugar-bush. Family Proteaceae. Found scattered on the lower mountain slopes, from Wemmershoek mountains to the Kogelberg and on to the Langeberg. The bracts are yellow with dense silky hairs. Flowers January–February.

Aulax pallasia, needle-leaf feather-bush. Family Proteaceae. Separate sex plants (male above). Grows up to 3 m. Found from Piketberg in the west to the Riviersonderend mountains in the east. Clusters of flowerheads, January–April.

THE SOMERSET WEST AREA

The cosmopolitan, fast-growing town of Somerset West (named after the autocratic Lord Charles Somerset, first governor of the Cape Colony) lies towards the eastern end of False Bay, below the splendid heights of the Hottentots Holland mountains. The latter are breached by the main N2 highway, which twists its dizzy way over the precipitous Sir Lowry's Pass. The views en route – blue ocean, white beaches, vineyard-graced hillsides and Table Mountain in the distance – are memorable.

The area's major attraction for flower lovers is the Helderberg Nature Reserve, a 360-ha expanse of species-rich countryside just to the north of Somerset West and set against a magnificent mountain backdrop: the area extends about half-way up the slopes of the high Helderberg, part of the Hottentots Holland range. Plant life embraces pelargoniums, ericas, proteas, an array of bulb-like plants and a myriad other species. Among the many birds that enchant the eye (one or two of which are found only in the region) are Victorin's warbler, red-chested flufftail, mountain buzzard and black eagle. Colour-coded circular walks encompass much of the terrain, the longest leading to Disa Gorge, where the land is mantled in wild flowers in high summer and early autumn. Other features of the reserve are pockets of indigenous forest (yellow-wood, stinkwood, ironwood, rooi-els), a number of antelope, a herbarium (comprising a library of dried plant specimens for reference), a shady picnic spot and a restaurant.

Just to the north of Somerset West is the Vergelegen homestead, one of the oldest and loveliest of the Cape Dutch country mansions. Completed in 1701 by W.A. van der Stel, the wildly extravagant Cape governor of the time, the estate was originally famed for its architectural beauty, its orchards, vineyards, orange groves and pastures, but thereafter suffered centuries of neglect before being restored by mining magnate Sir Lionel Phillips and his wife Florence. Vergelegen is now owned by the Anglo American Corporation.

It's spacious grounds are a delight, their focus the Octagonal Garden and its 300, mostly exotic flowering species. Other sections are dedicated to roses, herbs, a white garden and a shady tea garden. The estate's numerous fine tree specimens include five camphors planted by Van der Stel and a rare dawn redwood, a species that was, until fairly recently, thought to be extinct. The grounds and house are open to the public daily.

Calendar

Prime time for early spring flower-viewing is September to mid-October, but given the vast vegetation range there are always colourful or interesting plants to be seen – provided you're prepared to walk and search a little.

SPRING: Many annuals such as wild cineraria (*Senecio elegans*); Namaqualand daisies (*Dimorphotheca sinuata*) and all kinds of bulbs: babianas, gladioli, *Sparaxis*, lachenalias, *Moraea*, *Homeria*, *Ferraria*, *Romulea* and others; pelargoniums (especially *P. betulinum*); vygie shrubs such as *Ruschia* and *Lampranthus*; vaalkreupelhout (*Leucospermum conocarpodendron*) and other proteas, and the green snake-stem pincushion. In late spring one can see *Aristea*, orchids (*Satyrium* and *Corycium*) and varied disas.

SUMMER: Early summer brings out the everlastings (*Helichrysum*, *Syncarpha*); ericas in the uplands and in the flatland vleis of the Cape of Good Hope section of the Peninsula park;

A Cape sugar-bird seeks the nectar of a pincushion and, in return for the food, will pollinate the flowers.

lobelias; serrurias; a number of red flowering plants pollinated by the Mountain Pride butterfly: *Disa*, *Roella*, *Crassula coccinea* and *Tritoniopsis triticea*.

AUTUMN: Many bulbs, including *Haemanthus*, *Nerine*, the lovely March lily *Amaryllis belladonna*, *Brunsvigia*, *Boophone*, suurkanol (*Chasmanthe aethiopica*) and surings (*Oxalis*).

WINTER: The flowering bracts of *Leucadendron*; early winter brings *Oxalis* and the common pagoda (*Mimetes cucullatus*); proteas, including the common sugarbush (*Protea repens*); brownbeard sugarbush (*P. speciosa*); blackbeard sugarbush (*P. lepidocarpodendron*; and thistle sugarbush (*P. scolymocephala*); geelmagriet (*Euryops abrotanifolius*) a common winter-flowering shrub found on hill and mountain slopes.

For up-to-date information, call the MTN Flowerline 083 910 1028 (June to October).

The Cape Winelands

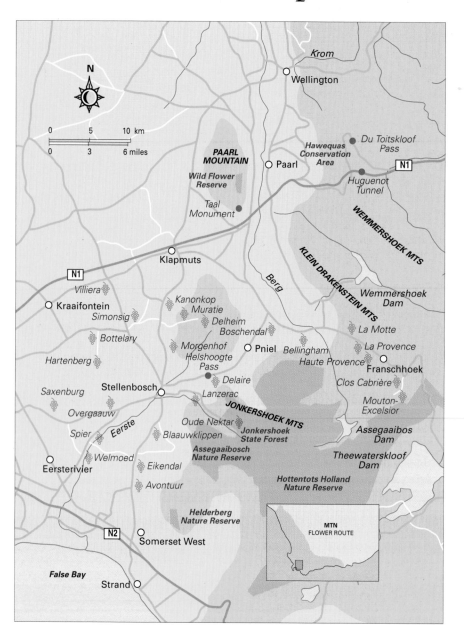

More than three centuries ago a handful of Dutch settlers left their small garrisoned outpost on the Cape Peninsula to farm a stunningly beautiful hinterland of high hills, green valleys and rich alluvial soils. Their move brought almost instant rewards: the new pastures nourished fat cattle to provide the small settlements with meat, milk and cheeses, and their wheat fields yielded such bounty that energies were soon turned to other, less essential crops – notably to the growing of wine grapes. By 1687 more than 400 000 vines had been planted and were thriving.

As the farmers prospered, so they enlarged their simple homes, adding wings and lofts and courtyards, a jonkershuis (the house reserved for the eldest son and heir), slave quarters for their growing labour force, coach-houses and stables and cellars to store their improving vintages. The architectural style that emerged, known and admired as Cape Dutch, contained elements borrowed from other places and cultures, among them medieval Holland, the Dutch East Indies and – following the arrival in 1688 of a group of Huguenot (Protestant) refugees – from France, but over the decades it developed its own, very distinctive character (see page 53).

The region now ranks as one of South Africa's premier tourist destinations. Its mansions, the high mountains, the vineyards, orchards and lush valley meadows all come together to create the most pleasing of environments, one that changes, quite delightfully, with the seasons. The evocative scents of maturing fruit fill the languid summer air; in autumn the colours soften to an infinite subtlety of ambers, russets and golds; in winter the peaks are mantled in snow; springtime brings the wild flowers. These last can be difficult to find and enjoy: the lowlands are intensively farmed and the uplands, which offer much more, can't really be explored unless you're a hiker. There are, however, some easily accessible nature reserves and a number of beautiful passes through the spectacular upland fynbos.

Basically, the region sustains two types of vegetation: mountain fynbos, and renosterveld on the richer shale and granite soils of the valleys – although, as noted, most of the land is under cultivation. Still, one can see patches of the latter here and there, small areas of natural vegetation dominated by renosterbos itself plus a profusion of bulbs such as moraeas, homerias, freesias, hesperanthas and romuleas.

Mountain fynbos grows on the Hottentots Holland, Stellenbosch, Jonkershoek, Franschhoek, Du Toit's Kloof and, most impressively, the Klein and Groot Drakenstein ranges. The extremely steep slopes, with their differing micro-climates and soils, nurture a spectacular array of ericas, proteas and restios (Jonkershoek Nature Reserve alone supports 1 142 species). Especially prominent are the hair-fringed cream or pink bracts of *Protea burchellii*; *P. neriifolia* near Jonkershoek; *Leuscospermum lineare*; *L. gueinzii*; the dark-red flowers of *Erica cruenta* or crimson heath; the common, widespread *Erica longifolia* with its green, red or pink flowers. There's also the highly colourful geelmagriet (*Euryops abrotanifolius*) and a variety of attractive everlastings (sewejaartjies).

THE WINE ROUTES

There can be few more pleasant ways of exploring the region than by one or other of its wine routes, sight-seeing and sampling itineraries modelled on France's famed *routes de vin* and the *Weinstrassen* of Germany. There are scores of wineries and estates that, between them, produce a vast selection of labels. The routes are well marked, the visits leisurely: one meanders from place to place through enchanting countryside, tasting the vintages, touring the cool, dim, wood-scented cellars, talking to the experts, perhaps staying to take lunch on a sun-dappled terrace. On some estates you'll find a small private museum; at others an art gallery, a gift shop, a farm stall that stocks fruit, vegetables, preserves and the delicious local cheeses.

Each of the four areas covered in this chapter – Stellenbosch, Franschhoek, Paarl and Wellington – has its own route. Stellenbosch's, the first to be established (in 1971), is the largest, taking in some 76 estates and co-operatives, all within easy reach of town; Wellington's is the youngest and smallest; all have produced award-winning wines.

STELLENBOSCH

This is the oldest of South Africa's country towns, founded in 1679 in the green and pleasant valley of the Eerste (first) River to the northeast of Cape Town and named in honour of Simon van der Stel, the able Dutch colonial governor of the time. The oak trees planted by the early inhabitants still grace the broad, quiet thoroughfares and much else of the elegant past remains – most visibly along Dorp Street and Die Braak, the original village green and festival-cum-parade ground. Dorp Street is flanked by the

THE FOUR PASSES

Perhaps the most rewarding of many scenic drives through the winelands and the surrounding countryside is the Four Passes circular route.

Start from Stellenbosch; take the R310 over Helshoogte Pass; turn right onto the R45 for the Franschhoek Pass (below), across the Franschhoek mountains and Hottentots Holland Nature Reserve (you'll see mountain fynbos, especially a wide variety of ericas, along the road through the higher parts) to Theewaterskloof dam and over Viljoen's Pass. The latter crosses the Groenlandberg (stunning views of mountain fynbos; masses of *Leucadendron laureolum*). On over the Hottentots Holland range via Sir Lowry's Pass, where much of the countryside has been restored by Cape Nature Conservation. Dense stands of *Protea repens* can be seen from the road along the lower slopes. Back over Sir Lowry's Pass and on to Stellenbosch.

country's longest row of historic buildings, among them Libertas Parva, a graceful, gabled Cape Dutch mansion that houses the Rembrandt van Rijn Art Gallery (on show are notable works by South African artists Irma Stern and Jacob Pierneef, and the sculptor Anton van Wouw). The cellar serves as the Stellenryck Wine Museum. Quite different in character is Dorp Street's Oom Samie se Winkel (Uncle Sammy's shop), an early trading store now rebuilt in period style and crammed to its eaves with local produce and collectables. Next door is De Akker, a popular pub with a wine library attached. Die Braak's buildings include the restored Burgherhuis (built in 1797 and filled with period furniture); the VOC-Kruithuis (the Dutch East India Company's powder-house and arsenal; built in 1777 and now a military museum); and the charming, thatch-roofed Anglican church of St Mary's-on-the-Braak (1852).

The Stellenbosch of yesteryear is perhaps even more vividly recalled in the Village Museum in Ryneveld Street, a collection of four venerable homes. The oldest of these, the Schreuderhuis, is a smallish cottage that dates from 1709. The historic houses are furnished in the styles of various periods, their gardens planted with the trees, shrubs and flowers that would have graced the originals.

Other Stellenbosch showcases celebrate the spirit of the vine, among them the Oude Meester Brandy Museum; the Bergkelder or mountain cellar, whose enormous vats are housed in chambers hollowed out of the Papegaaiberg hillside (tours and tastings); and the giant Stellenbosch Farmers' Winery. Opposite this last is the Oude Libertas amphitheatre, an entrancing venue for open-air Sunday shows: a picnic hamper, a bottle of good wine and a programme of music (or perhaps theatre or ballet) are the ingredients of a memorable evening.

Stellenbosch is a university centre, and its campus, integrated into the town, boasts some handsome buildings. Among them is its museum, which embraces an art gallery (in Dorp Street) and the respected Sasol art collection. The university also maintains *Hortus Botanicus*, a splendid botanical garden full of indigenous succulents, orchids, ferns, ancient cycads, bonsai, and the welwitschia, a remarkable species that grows in the near-barren wastelands of the Namib Desert and which the great Charles Darwin once described as 'the platypus of the plant kingdom'. Worth visiting, too, is the small Jan Marais Nature Reserve at the top of Merriman Avenue, haven to some lovely springtime wild flowers.

THE WIDER STELLENBOSCH AREA

Some of the most inviting of the region's estates and homesteads are clustered within a 12-km radius of town. They all produce good wines, some of them famous. Avontuur is known for its thoroughbred horses; Blaauwklippen for traditional Cape Malay relishes and preserves; Delaire, set high on Helshoogte Pass, enjoys superlative views; Muratie, renowned for its port wines, is among the oldest of the estates, dating back to 1685. The liveliest venue is perhaps Spier, whose lovely riverside gardens embrace a fine manor house (artworks on show), three restaurants (the Jonkershuis serves traditional Cape Malay fare), a wine centre, banqueting rooms, an amphitheatre for live music, theatre, opera and dance; delightful lakeside picnic spots, a farm stall, an equestrian centre (horseback rides around the vineyards) and a cheetah park. A novel and inviting

Oom Samie se Winkel ('Uncle Sammy's shop') is a charming reconstruction of one of Stellenbosch's earliest trading stores. The town, founded in 1679, has retained much else from its graceful past.

CAPE DUTCH ELEGANCE

The many lovely Cape Dutch homesteads that grace the Winelands are different in detail, but most have a number of elements in common. Among these are thick, lime-washed walls, a steeply pitched and beautifully thatched roof and pleasing symmetry, the latter created by a grand central entrance surmounted by a gable and flanked by evenly spaced, shuttered windows. The large and finely decorated gable – often the work of early slave craftsmen – is an especially distinctive element. Many houses also have gables at the sides and at the back.

way of getting to Spier is aboard the steam train that plies its venerable way from Cape Town station.

Pleasant digressions from the wine route include visits to the Jean Craig pottery studio on the Devon Valley road, where you can see fine craftware in the making; and Dombeya Farm, on the Annandale road and known for its hand-knitted products.

For nature lovers, an excursion to the Jonkershoek valley, east of Stellenbosch, is a must – not least for its renowned Lanzerac and Oude Nektar wine estates. The landscapes are superb, encompassing rivers and waterfalls and high flanking hills; walking trails have been charted, many of them wending their enchanting way to and through the 170-ha Assegaaibos Nature Reserve, haven for some rare proteas, various types of small buck and a number of unusual bird species. The lower parts of the reserve support renosterveld, the higher ones mountain fynbos. There are also small patches of forest comprising trees such as *Maytenus oleoides*, *Podocarpus latifolius*, and the bastard saffronwood (*Cassine peragua*). Next door is the Jonkershoek Forestry Reserve, also home to some lovely trees – and to large trout hatcheries.

Farther still to the east lie the spacious acres of the Hottentots Holland Nature Reserve, its 42 000 ha (which include the Jonkershoek Nature Reserve) embracing mountain peaks and rugged cliffs, ravines, rivers and deep-green woodland. Vegetation ranges from the moist fynbos of the low-lying areas to the wet, heath-dominated fynbos of the higher reaches. The lower-lying fynbos is dominated by proteas (*Protea repens*, *P. neriifolia* and others).

THE FRANSCHHOEK AREA

The charming little town of Franschhoek (French corner) was founded in 1688 by the first of the Huguenot settlers, refugees in search of sanctuary from the bitter religious wars of 17th-century France. These were skilled folk, some of them well versed in the sciences of viticulture and wine-making and, it transpired, with an educated eye for architectural beauty as well. Their vineyards and homesteads, many with Gallic names (Haute Provence, L'Ormarins, La Bri, La Motte among them)

Above: *The gazebo at Boschendal, near Franschhoek. The estate is famed for its sumptuous picnic hampers.*
Below: *Lanzerac, a splendid Cape Dutch manor-house built in 1830, now functions as a hotel and restaurant.*

still grace the exquisite Franschhoek and Drakenstein valleys, and most of them are accessible via the wine route known as Vignerons de Franschhoek. One of the most popular of the area's venues is Boschendal, an elegant Cape Flemish-style manor house renowned for the delicious traditional Cape buffet fare served in its restaurant. One can also eat in the shady grounds – from a sumptuous hamper provided by 'Le Pique-nique'.

The town is noted for its small, charmingly appointed haute cuisine restaurants and *auberges* (guest houses) and for the imposing Huguenot Memorial, centrepiece of the museum complex and set against a splendid mountain backdrop. The monument is full of imagery: its three arches represent the Holy Trinity; other features graphically symbolize faith, righteousness, religious freedom, the liberty of the spirit, agriculture and industry.

Above left: *This wine cellar, its surrounds garlanded with flowers, can be seen near Franschhoek.*
Above: *Part of the Jonkershoek valley, a place of river, waterfall and forest.*
Below: *The slopes of Paarl Mountain. A nature reserve, rich in bulbs and daisies, covers much of the hillside.*

THE PAARL AREA

Paarl, the largest of the region's towns – its tree-lined main street is fully 10 km long – began life in 1720 as a wagon-making and farming village, later featuring prominently in the long and eventually successful Afrikaans language movement. It is now a centre of the fruit canning, quarrying, tobacco manufacturing and, in particular, the wine industries.

This is an area of great beauty, of high mountain ranges mantled in the snows of winter and of fertile orchard-and-vineyard countryside cut through by the Berg River. The town itself is overlooked by the

FLORAL HIGHLIGHTS: THE WINELANDS

Homeria sp. Family Iridaceae. In southern Africa, there are about 30 of these small to medium-sized plants (maximum height 40 cm), found mainly in the southwestern areas. Many of the plants are poisonous to livestock (they are known as 'tulp'). The pink, yellow or cream flowers appear July–November.

Brunsvigia marginata. Family Amaryllidaceae. This bulb grows up to 20 cm in height on the mountain slopes around Ceres, Tulbagh, Worcester and Paarl. Its red flowers, borne on a compact head, are produced in March–June.

Leucadendron sessile, western sunbush. Family Proteaceae. This 1.5-m shrub's bracts are yellow or red. Male flowerheads are lemon-scented, females' are sweet-scented. Grows on granite clays on mountain slopes from near the coast to 600 m. Found on the Hottentots Holland and Witsenberg mountains, and from Elandskloof to Slanghoek. The flowers are produced in July–August.

Leucospermum lineare, needle-leaf pincushion. Family Proteaceae. A shrub growing up to 2 m tall and 3–4 m wide in dense stands on granite soils. Found on Hottentots Holland, and from Bainskloof to Du Toit's Kloof. Pale yellow to orange flowers are produced from July through to January.

Phylica pubescens, featherhead. Family Rhamnaceae. A 1.5-m shrub found in the Worcester and Stellenbosch areas and from the Cape Peninsula to Riversdale. Its white, feathery flowers appear in May–August.

Protea magnifica, queen protea. Family Proteaceae. A 2.5-m tall shrub that grows on hot, dry, very high mountain slopes. The large flowerheads are highly variable in form (cup- to bell- to bowl-shaped) and in colour (cream through to carmine). Flowers appear in June–January.

Protea burchellii, Burchell's sugar-bush. Family Proteaceae. The flowerheads of this 1–3 m tall shrub are shiny, cream to pink to carmine; margins have a white or a black beard. Grows on flats and lower slopes; Hottentots Holland to Olifants River and upper Breede River valley. Flowers June–July.

Erica longifolia. Family Ericaceae. This species varies from a fairly dense bush strewn with pink flowers to a lanky plant with yellow and brown flowers clustered at the end of its branches. The flowers are tubular and vary greatly in colour, from white through to yellow, green, pink, red and purple (and are even two-toned). Found on slopes; very common between Paarl and Bredasdorp, especially near Grabouw. Flowers at different times through the year but normally in the summer months.

Serruria rosea, rose spiderhead. Family Proteaceae. Shrub, about 1–1.5 m tall, with clusters of 15–20 pink, hairy-edged flowers that appear August–October. Found on sandstone sands, in dense stands, from Du Toit's Kloof to Hottentots Holland and Riviersonderend mountains.

Watsonia meriana, waspypie. Family Iridaceae. A bulb-like plant, 0.4–1.2 m tall, which bears red, pink or mauve flowers from September–October. It grows in damp sites, marshes and alongside streams, from Nieuwoudtville to Bredasdorp and is also found in Namaqualand.

dome-like immensity of Paarl Mountain (the world's second largest granite outcrop), named by an early traveller because its three globular, mica-studded summit peaks reminded him of gigantic pearls glistening in the dawn sunlight. There are superb views from the top: on the circular drive up you pass the Mill Water Wildflower Garden, a 15-ha place of fynbos (from other parts of the Western Cape), of proteas and gazanias, ericas and pincushions, and a joyful extravaganza of colour in springtime. The garden forms part of the 2 000-ha Paarlberg Nature Reserve, established on the mountain slopes to protect the area's renosterveld and fynbos. The reserve is especially rich in bulbs and daisies. These last bloom in spring, but whatever the season you'll find something in flower. Almost as attractive to nature lovers is the arboretum that sprawls along the Berg River bank near town: it embraces some 4 000 trees belonging to an impressive 700 different species. Here, too, is the Paarl Bird Sanctuary (136 species).

The most striking by far of Paarl's manmade structures is the Afrikaans language monument, or Taalmonument, a striking edifice on the lower slopes of the mountain. The memorial comprises three linked columns, a soaring spire and a fountain, and pays tribute to the various cultures that contributed to Afrikanerdom's linguistic heritage: African, European and Far Eastern. Among other Paarl showplaces are the Wagonmakers Museum; the beautiful Oude Pastorie, or Old Parsonage, which dates from 1786 and now functions as a museum of furniture and fine art; La Concorde, headquarters of the giant KWV, the world's largest wine co-operative, and Laborie, set on the hillside and noted for its restaurant (it serves traditional Cape dishes). The latter is atmospherically housed in an old wine cellar.

The area boasts some of the region's best-known cellars and wineries, including Backsberg, Fairview and, prince of estates, Nederburg, whose homestead, dating from 1792, hosts the annual and marvellously sociable Nederburg wine auction. Well worth visiting, too, is Paarl Rock Brandy Cellar, where you can view the entire brandy-making process. Quite different in its appeal is Nelson's

Creek estate, home to the Qunu African art, craft and entertainment centre. The Qunu complex (the name is taken from Nelson Mandela's Transkei birthplace) is a re-created Xhosa village; on offer are traditional Xhosa crafts, music, dancing, and the wisdom of the sangomas (spirit mediums).

East of Paarl is the Liemietberg Nature Reserve, a vast expanse of mountain countryside that sustains a splendid diversity of plants. In the Bain's Kloof and Du Toit's Kloof Pass areas you'll find *Protea laurifolia*, *Protea nitida*, yellow daisy (*Athanasia parviflora*) and a myriad restios.

Above: *The flowerhead of the well-known* Protea nitida *or waboom.*
Below: *Part of the 48-km, scenic Du Toit's Kloof Pass.*

THE WELLINGTON AREA

Sixteen kilometres to the north of Paarl, set on the banks of the Kromme River beneath the high Groenberg (green mountain), is the handsome little town of Wellington, a centre of South Africa's dried-fruit industry and of a rich fruit and winegrape countryside. The area has undergone several name changes since it was first farmed, in 1688, by the Huguenots. It was originally known as Liemiet Vallei (it lay at the outer limit of European settlement) and by the French as Val du Charron, later called Wagenmakersvallei (wagon-makers' valley) and finally, in 1840, renamed in honour of the Duke of Wellington, hero of the battle of Waterloo. Of note in town are the Huguenot College and the Old Blockhouse, the southernmost of more than 8 000 small forts built by the British in their expensive and generally fruitless effort to contain the Boer commandos during the South African War of 1899–1902.

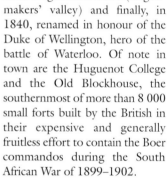

The road northeast from Wellington (the R303) leads you over the 30-km long, scenically superb Bain's Kloof Pass. Along the way there are fine views towards Paarl and Wellington; on the woodland summit is a picnic spot; the northward descent takes one through a deep ravine to a lovely land of river and waterfall. Highly recommended is the circular walk, starting from the Bain's Kloof forestry station, through rocky countryside of the Wolvens-kloof, an area rich in wild flowers.

Calendar

SPRING: The lower lying areas are best for the annuals: *Dimorphotheca*, *Arctotis*, *Ursinia*, *Senecio*, *Heliophila*, daisy bushes, *Athanasia*, *Othonna*, and pincushions. Also bulbs: irids, hyacinths, chincher-inchees (*Ornithogalum thyrsioides*) along the roadsides, where you'll also see lots of *O. dubium*. Varklelies grow in damp sites near farm dams.

SUMMER: This is often the peak flowering period in upper mountain areas, especially for ericas, lobelias and *Roella*.

AUTUMN: Scattered bulbs; amaryllids; *Brunsvigia*; *Haemanthus*, *Cyrtanthus* after fires.

WINTER: Proteas include *Protea neriifolia*, *P. repens*, *P. laurifolia* and *P. burchellii*. Early floral bracts of leucadendrons such as *L. laureoleum* and *L. xanthoconus*, can be seen in late winter and early spring

For up-to-date information, call the MTN Flowerline 083 910 1028 (June–October).

The Vergenoegd wine estate, one of the oldest in the Eerste River area.

The Breede River Valley

The Breede River rises in the high and scenically beautiful Ceres basin, gathers momentum as it flows through the precipitous Michell's Pass, runs between the Elandskloofberg and Witzenberg ranges and then swings southeast towards the towns of Worcester and Robertson. Mountains rise majestically on all sides, their winter heights covered in snow laid down by what are usually the Western Cape's heaviest falls. Often, the highest peaks are still wearing their white coats when the land far below is bright with the blooms of spring.

Ceres is named after the Roman goddess of agriculture, or abundance, and fittingly so: the valley of the Breede (broad) River is the largest and most productive of the wider region's fruit-growing areas – and, arguably, its most attractive. Various tributaries, most notably the 40-km long Hex River (whose valley is quite exquisite whatever the season) also sustain a splendid array of orchards and vineyards.

The upper region of the river comprises a series of basins bounded by sandstone heights which support mountain fynbos. Farming, however, has transformed the lower ground, and the riverbanks, especially between Ceres and Worcester, are infested with Australian black wattles and other aliens. Only tiny pockets of the original renoster-veld vegetation have survived. The area is still rich in bulbs, although, again, many are threatened with extinction. Below Michell's Pass the Breede River valley floor is covered in a mantle of alluvium – sand and pebbles – which once supported a form of fynbos but is now almost entirely occupied by fruit and vine plantings.

Around Worcester, the shale-covered hills are clothed in little succulent karoo – a sparse plant life noted for its vygies: low succulent shrubs, but also stonecrops (Crassulaceae), *Haworthia* and stapeliads. On the ancient termite mounds, known as heuweltjies, you'll find taller shrubs of gwarrie (*Euclea undulata*), *Rhus undulata*,

and bushier succulents such as aloes, *Euphorbia mauritanica* and botterboom (*Tylecodon paniculatus*). The shale at the base of the Langeberg and Riviersonderend mountains sustains renosterveld in a linking band between the little succulent karoo and the mountain fynbos (see also page 79).

THE TULBAGH AREA

Overlooked by three grand and well-watered mountain ranges (the Winterhoekberg, Witzenberg and Saronsberg), the picturesque town of Tulbagh lies some 15 km north-west of Ceres. The place was founded in the early 1700s, grew slowly and with grace, and now boasts the country's largest concentration of national monuments: Church Street alone is lined by more than 30 historic buildings, many of which were badly damaged in the great earthquake of 1969 (it measured 6.5 on the Richter scale and killed nine people). However, all the structures have been beautifully restored; several are worth a leisurely visit, among them the four that comprise the Oude Kerk Volksmuseum complex. Most prominent of the quartet is De Oude Drostdy, the

Above: *The Breede River in its middle reaches. Here one can clearly see the extent to which alien plants – Australian wattles and acacias – have invaded the Cape landscapes, which has led to degradation and the threat of flood damage.*
Opposite, top: *The common sunshine conebush,* Leucadendron salignum, *is a multi-stemmed shrub that grows in a variety of habitats ranging from the low-lying flats to the higher mountain slopes. It flowers between April and November.*

original magistrate's court and residence, which was designed by the renowned French architect Louis Thibault and now serves both as a rather lovely period museum and as headquarters of the local and most hospitable wine company.

Some 16 000 ha of surrounding mountain fynbos countryside, covering parts of the Koue Bokkeveld and Hawequas ranges, have been set aside as the Waterval Conservation Area. Here you'll find a wealth of mountain fynbos species: *Protea laurifolia*, *Protea nitida*, *Athanasia parviflora* (yellow daisy) and a multitude of restios. There are also patches of thicket featuring *Heeria argentea*, *Maytenus oleoides* and *Cassine peragua* trees. Wildlife includes klipspringer, baboon, jackal buzzard and black eagle.

THE CERES AREA

As charming a rural centre as Tulbagh, Ceres sits astride the Dwars River in a great, fertile bowl girded by the Witzenberg, Skurweberg and Hex River ranges. The basin ranks among the country's finest and most scenic fruit-growing areas, yielding vast quantities of peaches, pears, apples and nectarines. Among venues of interest in and around town are the Transport Riders' Museum (early wagons, carts and equipment)

Opposite page, top left: *The charming dewflower and the botterblom. The former, a vygie, has cascading magenta flowers that almost obscure the glittering succulent leaves during spring and summer. The botterblom is a daisy whose blooms appear at any time but mostly in the spring months.*

Below: *The mountain-flanked valley of the Hex River, one of the Breede's major tributaries. The valley's vineyards produce the greater part of South Africa's export grape harvest.*

and, to the south, the attractive 6 800-ha Ceres Mountain Fynbos Reserve. The latter embraces some rare plant species and a scatter of Bushman (San) paintings.

Wolseley, a small fruit canning and packing centre, lies to the southwest and is reached from Ceres via Michell's Pass, a spectacular route cut through a gap in a great mountain rampart, built by the renowned road engineer Andrew Bain and opened in 1848. It follows the path used by the transport riders of old (and also, since time immemorial, by migrating animals). Today the hillsides, cliffs and gorges of the wild country to either side attract hikers and climbers from afar. *Protea laurifolia, P. nitida* and a wealth of fynbos shrubs and restios decorate slopes which also support thickets of wild olive, Breede River yellowwood and other trees.

THE WORCESTER AREA

Perhaps even more dramatic than Michell's is the Hex River Pass, which opens the way through the mountains of that name. These lie to the south and east of Ceres, a rugged, in places precipitous and scenically stunning sandstone range whose highest point, the Matroosberg, rises 2 251 m above sea level. The snows of winter and good rains (over 1 500 mm a year) create a myriad swift-flowing streams.

The railway line north from Cape Town snakes its way up the slopes and over the pass. So, too, did the main highway – the N1, first stage of Cecil Rhodes's ambitious Cape-to-Cairo route – but most motorists now cut through the fairly recently built Huguenot Tunnel and miss much of the scenic splendour. Below the heights sprawls the Hex River valley, its flattish floor well irrigated, intensively cultivated, hugely productive – and visually quite enchanting, the summer greens softening to create a lovely tapestry of autumn and early winter colours. The valley encompasses some 200 farms which, between them, yield most of the country's export grapes.

Worcester, at the southern entrance to the pass, is a large town distinguished by its historic buildings, many of which flank Church Street. Other venues of note include Hugo Naude House (devoted to the works of this outstanding South African artist); Beck House, incorporating the Afrikaner Museum; and Stofberg House (local history). Just outside town is the Kleinplasie open-air working museum, a big and busy exposition of farm life past and present and a showcase for the region's produce and wines. The surroundings embrace a surprisingly extensive and, for the visitor, highly rewarding wine route; the KWV Brandy Cellar, in town, is the largest distillery of its kind in the world; daily tours of the cellar and its gleaming copper workings enable you to view the brandy-making process, and to sample the products.

SUCCULENTS ON SHOW

The countryside around Worcester occupies the western edge of the Little Karoo; of special interest to botanists is the Karoo National Botanic Garden, across the N1 to the north of town and known internationally for the number and variety of its succulents. On show are specimens endemic to the drier parts of the country; the cultivated section, which covers 10 ha of the 154-ha reserve, is cleverly organized, the plants grouped according to climate and area. Special displays feature, among much else, an array of bulbous species, carrion flowers and so on.

A view of the succulent karoo countryside around the town of Robertson. The area is noted for its vygies and stonecrops, for the sweet wines produced by its vineyards, and for the thoroughbred horses of its stud farms.

ROBERTSON TO MONTAGU

These two towns, set some 20 km apart, are centres of a wine industry famed for its sweetish, rather heavy vintages made from the musk-flavoured muscatel grapes grown in the region (Montagu holds the annual Muscatel Festival), and for its brandies and sherries. Among other features of the fertile and most attractive countryside are its fruit orchards and thoroughbred stud farms.

The Robertson area embraces three conservancies of special interest to flower enthusiasts. To the south of town is the Vrolijkheid Nature Conservation Station, a 2 000-ha expanse of low hills and gravel plains whose upper reaches sustain dry mountain fynbos and little succulent karoo plants. Prominent groups include vygies and stonecrops (Crassulaceae), *Haworthia* and stapeliads. You'll also see some aloes, and taller shrubs of *Euclea undulata*, *Rhus undulata* and botterboom. To the north, within a catchment area of the western Langeberg range, is the Dassieshoek Nature Reserve, a place of high mountains, cliffs, deep gorges, and a fine variety of mountain fynbos species, some of which are rare. Larger in extent but somewhat similar in character is

Erica cerinthoides, fire heath. Family Ericaceae: (erica or heath family). Probably the best known and most widespread erica species, found throughout South Africa. Varies in habit, size, shape and colour of flowers. It has tightly packed clusters of bright flowers (red in the Cape), which are tubular.

Erica monsoniana. Ericaceae (erica or heath family). A sturdy, erect and woody bush. Flowers are white tubes which open out, and are surrounded by spreading white parts giving a frilly effect. Grows on high mountains from Cederberg to Langeberg, but not Peninsula. Flowers October–February.

Podalyria biflora. Family Fabaceae (pea family). An erect, silky shrublet growing up to 60 cm tall on mountain slopes, and fairly widespread from Tulbagh to the Peninsula. The flowers are pink, occasionally white, appearing in October–December.

Sparaxis grandiflora, pers-kalkoentjie or witkalkoentjie (depending on colour). Family Iridaceae. A bulb-like plant found on clay flats from Clanwilliam to Peninsula to Caledon. The flowers, which may vary from white to plum-red, appear August–September.

Aloe ferox, bitter aloe. Family Asphodelaceae; related to the greater lily family. The plant's broad, fleshy leaves are dull green or reddish green with dark brown spines along the edges. The bright red or orange flower (rarely yellowish or white) is arranged in erect spikes. Found from Swellendam eastwards into KwaZulu-Natal, Lesotho and beyond. Known as 'Cape aloes', the leaves or roots, boiled in water, have a variety of medicinal uses. Flowers May–August.

Leucadendron chamelaea, Witsenberg conebush. Family Proteaceae. This shrub reaches up to 2.3 m in height. Male and female are separate plants; flowerheads of both have a pungent aroma. The plant has a fairly limited distribution, growing on level sandstone sands from the Ceres area to the Berg and Breede river valleys. The species is still common, but is classed as endangered in the Red Data Book due to threat from agriculture. Flowers appear in September.

Protea pityphylla, Ceres sugar-bush. Family Proteaceae. A sprawling shrub with a single trunk. Flowerhead is wine-red in colour, cup-shaped, nodding or on a stem curved like a swan's neck. Grows in small, isolated stands around Hex River mountains. Flowers May–September.

Top: *A pretty little cottage nestles in peaceful surrounds near Montagu. Among the town's attractions are its Mountain Nature Reserve, its historic buildings and its mineral springs.*
Above: *Montagu's spa complex.*

the Pat Busch private reserve, a 2 000-ha commercial farm (fruit, livestock) as well as a conservation area. The reserve lies among the foothills of the Langeberg, some 15 km from town. Cacti (from the Americas), aloes and other succulents are cultivated on the Sheilam farm, between Robertson and Ashton.

The road from Robertson to Montagu passes through the village of Ashton, known for its fruit canneries and enchanting rose nurseries, and for the Viljoensdrift wine-tastings and riverboat cruises. It then climbs up the 6-km, scenically spectacular Cogmanskloof Pass – a route that negotiates part of the Montagu Mountain Nature Reserve. This is a fine place for walking, and for enjoying the flora of the area – dry mountain fynbos on the lower slopes, moisture-loving plants at the upper levels, aloes and succulents on the steeper north-facing slopes. Species include waboom (*Protea nitida*), boegoekaroo (*Pteronia*), harpuisbos (*Euryops*) and the winter-flowering *Aloe ferox*.

Montagu itself has much to offer the visitor; major attractions are its historic buildings (one street alone is lined by 14 national monuments); its museum which features, among other things, a fascinating collection of herbs collected from the veld, and most especially its hot mineral springs, centrepiece of a pleasant resort complex. The spa's spring waters emerge at a constant 43° C. The civic gardens, which enclose a bird hide and a huge collection of mesembryanthemums, are well worth an hour or so of your time. A rather novel excursion is the tractor ride up the slopes of the Langeberg: fine views of the Robertson and Koo valleys unfold along the way.

Calendar

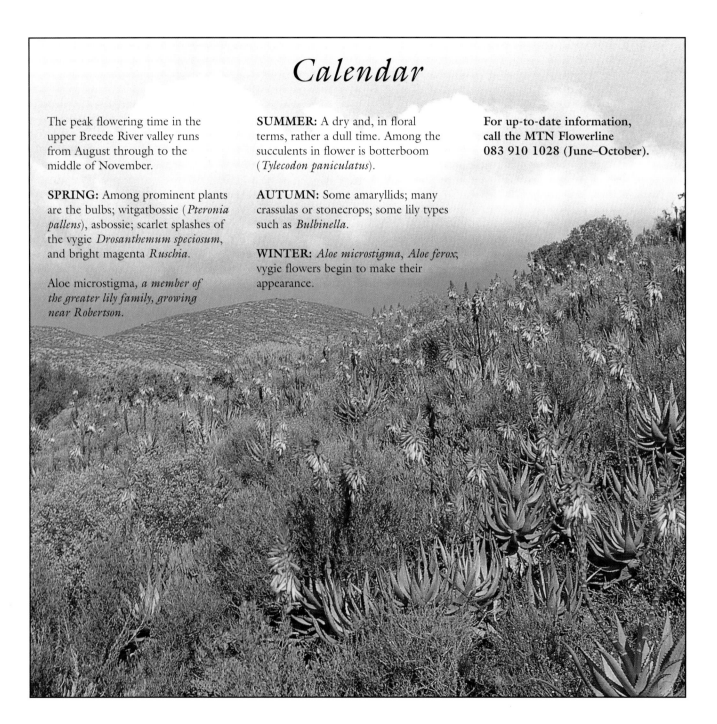

The peak flowering time in the upper Breede River valley runs from August through to the middle of November.

SPRING: Among prominent plants are the bulbs; witgatbossie (*Pteronia pallens*), asbossie; scarlet splashes of the vygie *Drosanthemum speciosum*, and bright magenta *Ruschia*.

Aloe microstigma, *a member of the greater lily family, growing near Robertson.*

SUMMER: A dry and, in floral terms, rather a dull time. Among the succulents in flower is botterboom (*Tylecodon paniculatus*).

AUTUMN: Some amaryllids; many crassulas or stonecrops; some lily types such as *Bulbinella*.

WINTER: *Aloe microstigma, Aloe ferox;* vygie flowers begin to make their appearance.

For up-to-date information, call the MTN Flowerline 083 910 1028 (June–October).

The Overberg

The hills of the Kogelberg, guardian of a biosphere reserve that sustains some 1 600 species of mountain fynbos, including 150 endemics.

*T*wo roads, both scenic delights, lead eastwards from Cape Town into the Overberg – a name, that, loosely translated, means 'the other side of the mountain' and refers to the coastal and hill countryside eastwards, beyond the Hottentots Holland range. The major route is the N2 highway that climbs the heights via Sir Lowry's Pass (see page 48) before descending, more gently, to and through a pleasant countryside of orchards, wheatfields and rich pastures. The minor route (though it is in excellent condition) hugs the Atlantic seaboard from Gordon's Bay to Hermanus before turning inland. The region is bounded in the north by the Riviersonderend and Langeberg ranges; its eastern extremity is the Breede River estuary.

The Overberg is blessed with remarkable floral variety: its western segment – the coastal stretch from Gordon's Bay to the Bot River and hinterland north to the Groenland mountain – has been internationally recognized as the Kogelberg Biosphere Reserve (one of the world's 330 areas registered as such by UNESCO under its Man and the Biosphere programme): a testament to the stunning diversity and large number of its flowering plants, many of which are found nowhere else in the fynbos biome.

The remainder of the region, by far the larger part, is almost as richly endowed with fynbos proteas, ericas and, especially, the russet restios that carpet the damp lowlands. You'll also find renosterveld on the richer shale soils of the rolling hills around Swellendam and Caledon, and small forest patches near Swellendam and Genadendal.

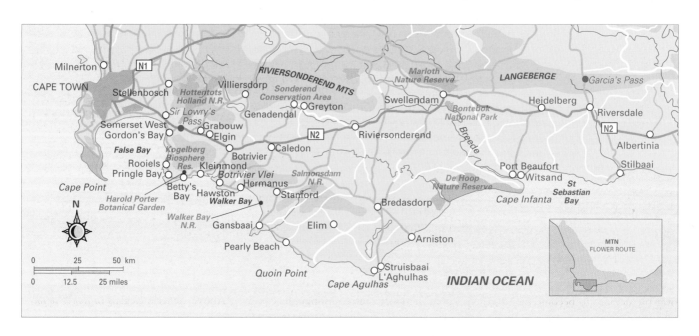

Summer winds bring rain from the warm Indian Ocean – rather more than the areas to the west receive – and this nurtures the bitter and krantz aloes that grow in the thickets. Wild gardenias with their scented, maroon-streaked, creamy-yellow flowers are common in the forests, which also give shade to the scarlet (or orange) tubular blooms of wild pomegranate. Kershout and sea guarri are trees of the coastal dune forests, and you'll see the occasional stately, umbrella-shaped milkwood on the coastal flats.

EAST OF PRINGLE BAY

The coastal route (Clarens Drive) winds along an attractive shoreline of cliff-girded coves, rivermouths and wide, sandy embayments that embrace pretty little bays and estuaries, resorts and residential villages. Among them are Rooiels, Pringle Bay, Hangklip, Betty's Bay, Kleinmond, the marshlands (or vlei) of the Bot River mouth (the town of Botrivier is some way upstream) and Hawston.

The drive south from Gordon's Bay to Pringle Bay – which, strictly speaking, is not part of the Overberg – is graced by mountain fynbos that comes right down to the road, providing an unusual opportunity to view the showy yellow flowers of the Overberg pincushion, the green tree pincushion (common in springtime) and other elements of somewhat rarefied vegetation.

Betty's Bay is known to flower enthusiasts for its Harold Porter National Botanic Garden, which contains a wealth of both coastal and mountain fynbos. Prominent are gladioli, watsonias, everlastings, the rare red disas and especially the ericas, of which more than 50 species are to be found within this small (188-ha) area. Five hectares of the garden are under cultivation, the plants helpfully labelled; mountain and other walks have been established, including an interpretive trail focusing on plant identification and the changing nature of the landscape. The main flowering season lasts from October to February, though the enchanting nerine lily blooms in March. Nearby Stony Point hosts one of only two mainland breeding sanctuaries for the endangered African (jackass) penguin.

Farther along the coast is the Kleinmond Coastal and Mountain Reserve (look out for *Erica pillansii*, unique to this particular corner of the biome), and the wetlands of the Bot River estuary, home to great numbers of waterfowl.

THE HERMANUS AREA

Set on the shores of Walker Bay, Hermanus is a one-time fishing village that has grown over the decades to become the Overberg's premier resort centre, distinguished by a fine new harbour that hosts both leisure and working craft, and by the rocky coves and

Top: *Part of the Harold Porter Botanical Garden near Betty's Bay.*
Above: Senecio elegans *in flower to the east of the seaside resort of Pearly Beach.*

KOGELBERG: A FANTASIA OF FLOWERS

The imposing Kogelberg range, inland from the stretch between Gordon's Bay and the Bot River estuary, is a prime venue for flower-hunters. The Kogelberg Conservation Area sustains around 1 600 mountain fynbos species, including 176 ericas and 150 endemics – plants that do not grow naturally anywhere else.

Most of the ericas are found at the highest levels; more easily seen are the profusions of Prince of Wales heath (*Erica perspicua*) that grace the lowland parts. These lovely blooms are popular among flower arrangers: colours range from white and pink 'sixpenny heaths' to the darker, white-tipped, scarcer upland 'ninepenny forms'.

Among the endemics is the exquisite, very rare marsh rose (*Orothamnus zeyheri*), a single-stemmed shrub with a pendulous head of rose-red bracts that grows on the moister middle and upper slopes. One needs to be fairly fit (and in possession of a permit) to explore these higher mountain reaches. Other species restricted to the area include the Kogelberg pagoda (subtle flowers nestle between up-curved orange-pink leaves), the matchstick pagoda (yellow and bright red flowers) and the conical pagoda (dazzling orange-red flowers).

Erica perspicua, Prince of Wales heath (left). Family Ericaceae. The translucent blooms are popular with flower arrangers for their lovely colours (white through to purple). Flowers February–June though some forms September–November.

Orothamnus zeyheri, marsh rose (left). Family Proteaceae. This lovely, tall, erect, rare plant can be seen in a few isolated stands. Flowers mainly in September.

Phaenocoma prolifera, rooi sewejaartjie (below). Family Asteraceae. A dense shrublet. Pink shading to red flowers bloom from September to April.

Brunia stokoei, rooistompie (above). Family Bruniaceae. A tallish shrub with large, slender red flowerheads. Flowers appear in November–April.

Mimetes hottentoticus, matchstick pagoda (left). Family Proteaceae. A rare shrub whose flowers, a mix of red and soft yellow, appear January–May.

Leucospermum oleifolium, Overberg pincushion (left). Family Proteaceae. A rounded shrub with turban-shaped flower-heads in pale yellow clusters (but crimson when mature). Flowers August–January but mainly September–October.

The Old Harbour at Hermanus, now a working museum.

golden beaches of its flanking seaboard. The backing cliffs provide pleasant walks and grand vistas. The town and its surrounds have much to offer the visitor (see box); Walker Bay is a prime whale-watching venue.

Some 1 500 ha of the Kleinrivier mountains above Hermanus are occupied by the Fernkloof Nature Reserve, whose terrain rises steeply from 60 to nearly 900 m to provide sanctuary for a splendid selection of mountain fynbos species. The reserve hosts the annual Hermanus Wild Flower Show. Some exquisite blooms can be seen along its 35 km of walking trails: its coastal frontage is graced by patches of milkwood, lemon-scented aasbos and the feathery-leafed, crimson-flowered *Erica plukenetii*. In summer the higher rocky outcrops are bright with scarlet klipblom; rather special is the heuningblom (*Retzia capensis*), a 2-m shrub with red, white-tipped tubular flowers and the sole member of the Retziaceae family.

Most of the bayshore and its immediate hinterland – the 15-km stretch running east from the bird-rich and beautiful Klein River estuary and lagoon – has been set aside as the Walker Bay Nature Reserve. Natural vegetation is dune fynbos; waxberry, bietou and sour fig are commonly seen. There are also thickets of milkwood. The Klipgat Cave, at the southeastern end, served as home to people of the Middle Stone Age (85 000 to 65 000 years ago) and is an important archaeological site.

Beyond, to the east, is Gansbaai, a substantial village which boasts a fishing harbour, some lovely flanking beaches and the Grootbos Private Nature Reserve, an area of limestone fynbos that sustains two special species (*Protea obtusifolia* and the silver-edge pincushion *Leucospermum patersonii*) and the endemic *Erica lineata*. Gansbaai rivals Hermanus as a whale-watching venue. Nearby is the well-named Danger Point, off which the *Birkenhead*, a British troopship, came to grief in 1852 with the loss of 445 lives. Those many soldiers and sailors doomed to die stood rigidly to attention while civilian passengers clambered aboard the only three lifeboats. Altogether, more than 250 vessels have been wrecked off this notoriously treacherous coast.

WHEN IN HERMANUS...

The Old Harbour tells the story of fishing and whaling over the decades; veteran and vintage craft on display. Here too there's a perlemoen (abalone) hatchery. Hermanus is the country's premier whale-watching venue and perhaps the most popular destination along the MTN Whale Route. Southern rights come inshore to breed and calve in Walker Bay between June and November; numerous vantage points, including the high backing cliffs, provide rewarding shore-based observation. The town's whale crier (the only one in the world) alerts passers-by to the presence of these giant marine mammals (below). The annual Whale Festival (music, dance, drama; exhibitions of arts, crafts, flowers) takes place over eleven days in October.

INLAND TO CALEDON AND GREYTON

Hot springs and their curative properties prompted the founding of Caledon in the early 18th century (a local landowner started a kind of health farm as early as 1709). It's still a popular spa town, but now has a lot more to offer visitors – especially those who love flowers.

Among the most attractive corners of the entire region is the Caledon Nature Reserve and Wild Flower Garden, a smallish expanse of Swartberg hillside whose 56-ha cultivated section has been beautifully landscaped. Its myriad fynbos residents include the entrancing Caledon bluebell (*Gladiolus bullatus*); pathways meander over wooden bridges and past stands of indigenous forest; a 10-km trail takes you through the wider area. The annual Caledon Wild Flower Show, held in mid-September, ranks among the most important and colourful of the country's floral expositions.

Some 50 km to the southeast (take the R316, and turn right onto the R326 towards Stanford) is the ruggedly scenic, 850-ha Salmonsdam Nature Reserve, a fine place for flower-watching, bird-spotting (124 recorded species) and communing with nature. The lower slopes are scattered with proteas; the highest parts support ericas; patches of forest grace the valleys; and one can see many wetland and riverine plants. Five trails, ranging from three to nine kilometres, have been established.

The pleasantly embowered village of Greyton, beyond the N2 to the northeast of Caledon, is favoured by the quieter Capetonian weekender for its rather old-world charm, its three hotels (among them the celebrated Post House, built and furnished in English Country style) and for the tranquility of its surroundings. The place slumbers in the shadow of the Riversonderend range, the southern slopes of its 2 200-ha nature reserve covered by wet mountain fynbos. Ericas are notable at the higher elevations. Farther into these mountains, and extending over neighbouring ranges, is the much larger (26 000-ha) Sonderend Conservation Area, best explored via the Boesmanskloof and Genadendal hiking trails. Dominant vegetation here, again, is wet mountain fynbos, though you'll find some succulent karoo scrub on the north-facing slopes.

When in the Greyton area, make a point of visiting Genadendal, a timeless little settlement of thatched cottages set in the 'vale of peace' to the west. The village, the country's first mission station, was founded in 1737 and has hardly changed since. Farther west (though not directly linked to Greyton) is Villiersdorp, whose several attractions include an exquisite wild flower garden laid out on the slopes of the Aasvoël Mountain.

THE SWELLENDAM AREA

The town of Swellendam is both historic and handsome: it started life more than 250 years ago and, apart from a brief attempt at rebellion in the 1790s (it declared itself an independent republic), grew peacefully, and gracefully, over the centuries. Especially notable is its beautiful drostdy, the early (1747) magistrate's court and residence which now serves as the centrepiece of a museum complex. Other notable buildings

Above: *The charming village of Greyton, overlooked by the Riviersonderend mountains, boasts three good hotels and an attractive nature sanctuary.*
Below: *Swellendam's historic drostdy, or early magistrate's court, now forms part of a museum complex. In the Langeberg range to the north of town is the ruggedly beautiful Marloth Nature Reserve.*

Calendar

SPRING: Mid-September to mid-November is the prime viewing period: pincushions are in full show; proteas at the tail end of their flowering season; bulbs; some annuals, but the displays are not as impressive as those to the west of the Hottentots Holland range. Ponds and dams are often covered in the white, scented blooms of waterblommetjies, an important ingredient of a traditional Cape stew.

SUMMER: The flowers, notably a profusion of ericas, are at their best in the higher parts of the Kogelberg, Langeberg and Riviersonderend mountains.

AUTUMN: This is the best time for amaryllids and bloedblom (blood flower), a brilliant red 'paintbrush' that decorates the coast.

WINTER: The season for proteas and initial leucadendrons.

For up-to-date information, call the MTN Flowerline 083 910 1028 (June to October).

The Aspalathus excelsa *shrub grows on coastal flats, and on the lower slopes around Caledon.*

Agathosma serpyllacea, buchu. Family Rutaceae. A low shrub with white, pink or mauve flowers that appear in clusters at any time of year. The plant grows on coastal or inland sand, and on limestone flats and slopes from Clanwilliam right through to Mossel Bay.

Erica oblongiflora, 'sticky green heath'. Family Ericaceae. A straggling shrub that branches out in all directions, and grows on the limestone outcrops of the hills and old dunes to the south-west of Bredasdorp. Greenish-yellow flowers, which are some-what sticky, appear April–July.

Aspalathus pycnantha. Family Fabaceae. A shrublet that grows to 15–50 cm in height on the coastal flats and slopes around Bredasdorp. Its pale yellow flowers bloom from July to October.

Erica regia. Family Ericaceae. A shrub that has tubular, strikingly red, sticky flowers. It grows in stony ground near Elim. A popular garden plant. Also popular is a form, known as 'Elim heath', which has a white flowertube ending in a green then red tip. Flowers thoughout the year, peaking in spring.

Erica bruniades. Family Ericaceae. A slender shrublet that grows up to 45 cm in height, the pale pink to rosy petals barely protruding from their white, shaggy-haired surrounds. It grows in damp soil near streams. Widespread, and common, from Vanrhynsdorp to Peninsula and east to Bredas-dorp. Flowers July–January.

Euchaetis longibracteata. Family Rutaceae. A shrub that grows up to 80 cm in height, found on the limestone hills around Bredasdorp and in the Swellendam area. The white flowers appear December–April.

Erica mariae. Family Ericaceae. A variable shrub (according to habitat): 2 m tall, woody and lanky on the Potberg sandstone but only 90 cm on limestone. Narrow distribution along coast from De Hoop to Stilbaai. The flowers, dark red and somewhat sticky, appear January–March.

Gazania pectinata. Family Asteraceae. A shrublet that grows either as an annual or a perennial on coastal flats and the lower slopes from Hopefield through to the Cape Peninsula and on to Caledon and Bredas-dorp. Yellow or orange flowers appear in August–November.

FLORAL HIGHLIGHTS: THE OVERBERG

Moraea insolens.
Family Iridaceae. A bulb-like plant, reaching 20–35 cm in height, that grows on the clayey south-facing slopes around Caledon. The orange or cream flowers appear in September.

Struthiola argentea, aandgonna. Family Thymelaeaceae.
A shrublet that grows to 60 cm in height on coastal flats or lower slopes from Stellenbosch eastwards, to Oudtshoorn, Caledon, Port Elizabeth and beyond. The yellowish flowers are produced in May–December.

Leucospermum truncatum, limestone pincushion. Family Proteaceae. A rounded shrub with a hairy, golden yellow to orange flowerhead. The plant grows in dense, isolated stands on limestone soils on the flats and lower slopes in the Soetanysberg area. Flowers are produced in August–December.

Roella rhodantha.
Family Campanulaceae.
A sprawling shrublet growing up to 20 cm in height on the rocky mountain slopes near Bredasdorp. The red or pink flowers are produced in November–January.

Leucospermum cordifolium, pincushion. Family Proteaceae. A rounded shrub. Flowerhead has yellow or orange or crimson parts. Grows at low altitudes from Kleinmond and Houhoek Pass to Bredasdorp, Elim flats and Caledon. The classic pincushion, used in many popular hybrids. Flowers August–January.

Protea denticulata, tooth-leaf sugarbush. Family Proteaceae. A shrub, up to 1 m in height, that grows only on the Potberg (in the De Hoop Nature Reserve). The flowerhead is about 4 cm long and 4 cm across, with dull reddish bracts that are dense with hairs. The flowers are produced in August–October.

Syncarpha argyropsis, witsewejaartjie. Family Asteraceae. A shrublet that grows 30–70 cm in height from Caledon to Riversdale. The leaves are silvery. The white, papery flowers are produced in September–December.

Protea compacta, Bot River sugarbush. Family Proteaceae. A lanky, sparsely branched shrub, found in large dense stands on sandy soils at low levels near Kleinmond, on the Bredasdorp mountains and the flats towards the sea. Pink or white flowers appear in April–September.

Above: *The leopard tortoise, a resident of the Bontebok National Park near Swellendam.*
Below right: *One of the fishermen's cottages that grace Struisbaai. The seaside hamlet lies just to the east of Cape Agulhas, Africa's most southerly point.*

FLOWERS FOR SALE

The Overberg's floral riches are big business: the Elgin Valley alone supplies 40 per cent of the Western Cape's cut flowers. Proteas, ericas and other fynbos plants are farmed for both the export and domestic markets; much else is harvested from the natural veld, some of it to meet the demand for dried flowers. Moreover, the fine foliage of many of the species provides the 'greens' for the cut-flower trade. In all, the industry gives employment to some 20 000 people in the Western Cape. The Overberg is a major source of reeds for roof-thatching, an ancient craft nurtured in Elim and other mission-related villages.

include the Old Gaol and the venerable post office next door (the original jailor doubled up as postmaster); the watermill (which still grinds flour); and the trades yard (ambagswerf), a cluster of re-created craftsmen's premises.

Swellendam lies beneath the Clock Peaks – so called because one can tell the approximate time of day from the shadows they cast – of the scenically splendid Langeberg range, some 11 000 ha of which have been set aside as the Marloth Nature Reserve. Here, day walks (and the five-day Swellendam Hiking Trail) take one through fynbos and forest. The lower slopes are dominated by tall, dense fynbos with protea stands (narrow-leaf sugarbush *Protea neriifolia*); buttery-yellow bracts of gum-leaf conebush can be seen on the forest margins; various ericas grow on the higher slopes (note, especially, the minute rosy-pink to red flowers of *Erica hispidula*). Trees include Outeniqua and true yellowwood, kershout, Cape beech and rooiels. A similar wealth of mountain fynbos, and one of the region's most extensive patches of indigenous forest, can be found in the slightly larger Boosmansbos Wilderness Area to the east.

A conservation area quite different in character is the Bontebok National Park, sited in flattish countryside 7 km south of town. The reserve was originally established (in 1931) near Bredasdorp to protect the pitiful 20 or so of these medium-sized, vari-coloured antelope that had managed to survive the hunter's gun and encroaching farmland. It was later moved to its present location, and the bontebok have flourished. Animals, though, are by no means the only attraction: the park is almost as well known for its trees and flora, including wild olive, milkwood, Breede River yellowwood, and renosterveld and grassy fynbos; some of the nearly 500 plant species are rare, a few of them showy. The wart-stemmed pincushion can be seen year-round; the creamy flowerheads of *Leucospermum calligerum* are prominent in spring. Redgrass (good for grazing) is common among the fynbos.

SOUTH TO AGULHAS

Cape Agulhas, southernmost extremity of the African continent and the true meeting point of the Indian and Atlantic oceans, is scenically unremarkable: it's at the end of a gently sloping inland plain that slips quietly into the sea to become the great, shallow Agulhas Bank. The cape's most striking feature is its lighthouse, built in 1848 in the style of the famed Pharos light-tower near Alexandria in ancient Egypt. A section of the interior is devoted to the story of lighthouses past and present, the whole forming part of Bredasdorp's fascinating Shipwreck Museum complex.

Close to the cape are the two hamlets of L'Agulhas and Struisbaai, from where a splendid beach stretches towards Arniston.

The latter, also known as Waenhuiskrans (wagon-house cliff, a reference to a nearby sea-cavern), is a picturesque little place of lime-washed fishermen's cottages whose English name is taken from one of the many shipwrecks recorded along these often treacherous shores. The *Arniston*, a troopship, foundered in 1815 with the loss of 372 lives, most of them British soldiers.

Some way along the coast to the east of Arniston lies the De Hoop Nature Reserve, a 36 000-ha expanse of huge, white, shifting dunes and of wetland, hill and mountain (the Potberg range extends into the area) that supports an impressive 1 500 plant species (50 of them endemic) and is considered a 'hot spot' of plant diversity. For the most part the terrain is covered in limestone fynbos – known for the strong scents of its buchu plants (which belong to the citrus family) – with some dune fynbos and patches of milkwood forest. Notable are the limestone sugarbushes, limestone conebushes, silverball conebushes, limestone pincushions and the creamy white flowers of *Erica spectabilis*. The upper slopes of the Potberg are clothed in tolbos and silver pagoda proteas; the midslopes host the reddish-carmine flowers of the tooth-leafed sugarbush, a Potberg endemic. Also in residence are Cape mountain zebra, a number of antelope and the region's last breeding colony of the rare Cape vulture. De Hoop's marine reserve is one of the premier breeding grounds of the southern right whale.

Bredasdorp, 25 km to the north of Agulhas, is the district's main town, a fairly substantial farming centre whose Mountain Reserve, and especially its cultivated section, is noted for ericas, proteas and the blood-red Bredasdorp lily (*Cyrtanthus guthrieae*). An especially rewarding excursion is that to Elim, 37 km to the southwest. This, like Genadendal (see above, page 72), has remained virtually unchanged since it started life in the 1830s as a Moravian mission station. Of interest are the hamlet's watermill, oldest of its kind in the country (1828) and its church clock (dating from 1764 and still keeping good time). The fynbos of the area is so special that it has been accorded its own name: Elim fynbos. Elim heath (*Erica regia*), which is also notable, produces its tubular, white, crimson-tipped flowers throughout the year. Restios are common; proteas are sparse; the Elim conebush, rough-leaf cone-bush and Bredasdorp conebush are threatened by farming activity. However, the Geelkop Nature Reserve, a community initiative, offers a honeypot of local endemics, among them yellow-green trident pincushions and deep-pink bashful sugarbushes (*Protea pudens*), which have bell-shaped flowerheads. In springtime the countryside to the south is decorated with the pink and yellow blooms of the oval-leaf pincushion and, in the rockier parts, the classic pincushion with its yellow-orange flowerheads.

Top: *Fishing boats drawn up on the beach at Arniston.*
Above: *The Cape mountain zebra, once a seriously endangered species, flourishes in the De Hoop Nature Reserve.*

The Klein Karoo

For the most part the region, also known as the Little Karoo (and as 'Kannaland', after the vygie-type kannagoed plant), comprises a broad, 250-km long plain flanked by grand ranges: the Langeberg and the Outeniqua mountains to the south, and the high, rugged and scenically magnificent Swartberg to the north.

The Klein Karoo, despite its name, is very different in character from the vast, semi-arid Great Karoo that sprawls away across the country's south-central interior. Rainfall is modest enough, averaging just 150 mm or so a year, but the land is nurtured by the many perennial streams that flow down from the high mountains, and which have enriched the soil with the alluvial deposits they bring. The valleys of the Olifants River and the smaller watercourses are fertile, sustaining wheat, grapes, tobacco, walnuts, deciduous fruit orchards and great fields of emerald lucerne. This is also ostrich country: in late Victorian and Edwardian times Oudtshoorn, the region's principal town, fed the fashion-led demand for ostrich feathers and, although the boom was brief and the industry declined, nearly 100 000 of these big birds are still farmed in the area.

Plant life is both distinctive and prolific, falling within four main vegetation types. The higher ranges are typical mountain fynbos terrain, supporting a wealth of proteas, ericas and restios. On the western

Above: *The Klein Karoo is rich in fossil plant traces.*
Opposite: *A typical Klein Karoo landscape. The countryside, dry though it appears, is nurtured by perennial streams that tumble down from the mountains.*

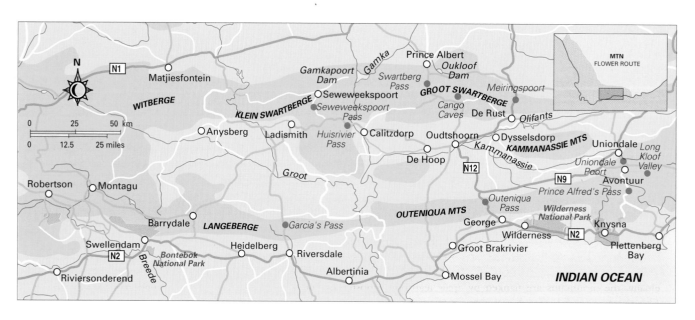

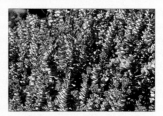

Crassula rupestris, bergkraaltjies. This shrub's leaves come in attractively varied colours: individuals may be green, yellow, orange coral, dark red or outlined with a darker tone. White or pink flower clusters appear May–August.

Glottiphyllum fergusoniae. Family Mesembryanthemaceae. A 'mesemb' that forms clumps of irregular, star-shaped leaves, succulent and soft to the touch. Its fairly large, striking flowers are produced in March and April.

Tylecodon cacalioides, nenta. This succulent, found from Ladismith to Uniondale, has bright yellow flowers in December–February.

lowlands (and especially around Oudtshoorn and between Barrydale and Ladismith) you'll find plants of what is known as the Little Succulent Karoo, among them *Haworthia viscosa* – a curious species, notable for its pink tubular flowers and attractive leaves – and vygies in such number and variety that the countryside is eerily reminiscent of Namaqualand, far to the northwest. Of note are the quartz gravel fields that stretch in a band from Anysberg southeastwards: they look lifeless, but many of the gravel-like 'quartz stones' are in fact tiny succulents in camouflage. The tall, slender shrubs of klapperbos (Chinese lantern) along the roadsides are rather dull for most of the year, but delight the eye with their bright lantern-like pods in late spring and early summer. Thirdly, there is the spekboomveld, named after the predominance of a hardy succulent-leafed shrub whose dense, pink blossoms cover parts of the land in October and November. Rising above the spekboom mantle between May and August are the magnificent red spires of the bitter aloe (*Aloe ferox*; see box, page 82); less striking but lovely nevertheless are the pinkish-red, clustered flowers of *A. striata*, the coral aloe, which blooms between July and October.

Finally, the mountains are flanked by areas featuring renosterbos and a modest complement of bulbs (springtime viewing).

THE CALITZDORP AREA

Ladismith, a pretty, rather old-fashioned little town set 45 km west of Calitzdorp, is distinguished by its scenic setting beneath the high Swartberg, by its apricot trees (vast numbers are grown in the Hoeko valley to the east), by the quality of the local wines and cheeses, and by the area's Towerkop Conservation Area, a rugged expanse of highland countryside that takes its name from the soaring peak to the north of town. The Seweweekspoort ('seven weeks poort') peak rises to 2 325 m above sea level and dominates the gravelled route of the same name, an aloe-fringed throughway girded by gigantic, orange-hued sandstone cliffs. Notable plants here include the blood-red Ladismith sugarbush (*Protea aristata*) which, unusually, produces its flowers in summer. To the south of town is the 2 770-ha Ladismith-Klein Karoo Nature Reserve, haven to an array of hardy succulent karoo shrubs such as botterboom, which looks a bit like a miniature baobab but produces red tubular flowers on graceful stems. Among especially striking shrubs or trees are *Crassula arborescens*, with its silver, red-edged leaves and massed white flowers changing to pink, and the variously coloured bergkraaltjies.

Worth a digression west from Ladismith is the 36 000-ha Anysberg Nature Reserve, whose quartz fields are scattered with miniature succulents. There's renosterveld on the apronland and mountain fynbos higher up. Several of the reserve's plant species, including two rare ericas, are endemic.

The road east from Ladismith (the R62) cuts through the scenic Huis River Pass before descending to the Gamka River valley and to Calitzdorp, centre of a prosperous farming region, of the ostrich-farming industry, and of a wine route. The local grapes have a high sugar content. Travellers negotiating the pass are treated to fine displays of pink-flowered spekboom.

Some 20 km from town, on the banks of the Olifants River, are the healing mineral springs of the Caltizdorp Spa.

ACROSS THE SWARTBERG

The massive heights of the Swartberg are breached by the splendid Swartberg Pass. The route was built – by the celebrated road engineer

Above: *The snow-capped heights of the Swartberg range overlook rich farming country along the way from Calitzdorp to Oudtshoorn.*
Below: *Part of the scenic Swartberg Pass between Oudtshoorn and the Great Karoo village of Prince Albert.*

Thomas Bain (with the help of convict labour) in the 1880s – to link Oudtshoorn with the Great Karoo village of Prince Albert, twisting its way up to the 1 585-m summit and then down the other side through 24 km of sharp curves and steep gradients. The vistas are spectacular; the mountain slopes, decorated with ericas and watsonias, are a joy in summer; leucadendrons and sugarbush proteas enliven the winter landscapes, when heavy snowfalls occasionally close the route. A few kilometres from the top a road branches off to Gamkaskloof (known as De Hel, incorrectly translated as 'The Hell'), a massive gorge that accommodates the Gamka River and its once isolated and fertile valley.

Prince Albert, founded in 1762, is a tranquil little town noted for its Karoo-style, Cape Dutch and Victorian architecture, its historic water mill and the brief, animated part it played in the country's gold-mining story (the diggings proved uneconomic; relics of the gold-rush are on display in the local museum). To the west is the Gamkapoort Nature Reserve, a grand 8 250-ha expanse of little succulent karoo vegetation, stands of sweetthorn trees along the banks of the Gamka and Dwyka rivers and, in the high parts, dry mountain fynbos. Access is rather difficult; one needs an entry permit.

THE OUDTSHOORN AREA

The town, largest in the Klein Karoo, has been known as the world's 'feather capital' ever since the leaders of late Victorian society, taking their inspiration from the Art Nouveau movement, set the fashion for flowing lines and fulsome accessories. The boom, which lasted for about two decades, made instant millionaires of the local ostrich farmers (at one time London buyers were paying more than £100 for a pound of quality white feathers), the wealthiest of whom built palatial homes for themselves – marble-floored, turreted, elaborately decorated extravaganzas that proved too costly to maintain when the market finally collapsed.

SHOWPLACES AROUND OUDTSHOORN

Ostrich farms are still very much a feature of the Oudtshoorn countryside, though the big birds are now reared for their hides and meat as well as their feathers. The latter are used, for the most part, in the manufacture of feather dusters. Three of the local farms – Highgate, Cango and Safari – offer guided tours. Other drawcards in the area are the Cango Wildlife Ranch, the Cango Butterfly Farm, the Cango Angora show-farm – and most especially, the recently upgraded Cango Caves (below).

The cave complex, an enormous labyrinth of limestone chambers, passages and spectacular, multi-hued dripstone formations, lies on the southern slopes of the Swartberg 26 km north of Oudtshoorn. In fact there are five sequences. Cango One, the first to be 'discovered' (by a local herdsman in 1780; long before, it had served as home to people of the Middle Stone Age and to Bushman hunter-gatherers), comprises 28 chambers, including one, the Grand Hall, which is 16-metres high and more than 100 m across. Cango Two, found by cave guides in 1970, is known as the Wonder Cave for its fantasia of sculpted stalagmites and stalactites. Cangos Three, Four and Five are said to be even bigger and more beautiful but difficult to access, and remain closed to the public. Visitor facilities include three different guided tours, a restaurant, crèche and gift shop.

Top: *One of Oudtshoorn's elaborate and historic 'feather palaces'.*
Above: *The delicate flowers of* Brunsvigia striata.

A few of the mansions, though, have survived the years, including Pinehurst (not open to the public), and the town's C.P. Nel Museum and its annexe (the beautifully designed Dorpshuis). The museum's Ostrich Room is well worth a visit for its evocative displays of the romantic past and insight into an industry that, though now much quieter than in its heyday, continues to flourish.

THE ROAD TO UNIONDALE

The route eastwards takes you along the Olifants River valley, initially to the picturesque village of De Rust, at the entrance to Meiringspoort. The latter is a 13-km highway cutting through towering sandstone cliffs; close to its northern end is a grand, 55-m high waterfall. To the south of the R341, occupying much of the land between Oudtshoorn and Uniondale, lies the Kammanassie Nature Reserve, a 28 000-ha sanctuary that embraces the rugged Kammanassie mountains, their deep gorges and their mountain fynbos, spekboomveld and renosterveld vegetation.

THE FAR EAST
The town of Uniondale, at the far eastern end of the Klein Karoo, was once prominent in the wagon-building and ostrich-farming industries, but has now settled into quieter routines. Among local attractions are the water mill, scheduled for conversion into an art gallery and museum; an especially rewarding drive is that which leads you south, over Uniondale Poort to Avontuur and the fruit orchards of the fertile, and very lovely, Long Kloof valley.

WEALTH FROM BITTER ALOES
Among the more commercially valuable of the Klein Karoo's plants is the bitter aloe (*Aloe ferox*), the major ingredient of a dark-brown, resinous substance – 'Cape Aloes' – employed in the treatment of stomach ailments and as a laxative or purgative. Most of the product is exported to Europe, together with juice from the leaves. The fleshy part of the leaf is also the source of aloe gel (or rather, a local version of the gel), which is used in the cosmetics industry.

Calendar

SPRING: Depending on rains, enchanting floral displays in the little succulent karoo: of perennial shrubs such as witgatbossie, with orange flowerheads and leaves; asbossie (yellow daisy-like flowerheads); oranje gousbloom (*Gazania krebsiana*) and other low herbs; annuals (leeubekkies); vygies and bulbs. Geelberggranaat, a 2-m shrub with fragile yellow flowers, puts on a stunning show.

For up-to-date information, call the MTN Flowerline 083 910 1028 (June to October).

SUMMER: Overall, not really a good time for flowers, but in some instances entire slopes are covered in flowering spekboom; and the brilliance of boerboon can enliven otherwise dull landscapes. Attractive displays of ericas at the top of Swartberg Pass; Ladismith sugarbush produces large crimson, goblet-shaped blooms from October to February, peaking in December.

AUTUMN: Mainly amaryllids, *Brunsvigia*, *Haemanthus*, and crassulas.

WINTER: Proteas can be seen on the higher ground; aloe species on the lower ground and in the spekboomveld; sorrel (*Oxalis*), and some early bulbs.

The flowers of rhe boerboon, blooming in dense clusters, are a familiar sight from Montagu east to Oudtshoorn. from January through to April.

FLORAL HIGHLIGHTS: KLEIN KAROO

Pteronia incana, asbossie. Family Asteraceae. A highly branched shrub, 0.5–1 m tall, with grey leaves. The plant grows in a variety of habitats; it is widespread in the Klein Karoo, Great Karoo, northwest up to Namaqualand and eastwards to the Eastern Cape. The yellow flowers appear August–October.

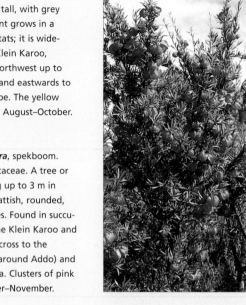

Nymania capensis, Chinese lantern, also known as klapperbos. Family Meliaceae. A shrub or small tree that grows to 4 m. The species is at its most striking when in fruit, with its pinkish, inflated pods resembling small lanterns. It is found in arid areas in the Klein Karoo, in the Eastern Cape and up to Namibia. The red or pink flowers appear at various times depending on habitat but broadly from October to December.

Portulacaria afra, spekboom. Family Portulacaceae. A tree or shrub, growing up to 3 m in height, with flattish, rounded, succulent leaves. Found in succulent scrub in the Klein Karoo and Humansdorp across to the Eastern Cape (around Addo) and in Mpumalanga. Clusters of pink flowers October–November.

Dicoma picta, knoppiesdoringbossie. Family Asteraceae. A tall (30–60 cm) shrub, twiggy in form, which grows on stony slopes from Uitenhage in the east through to George, the Cederberg, Great Karoo and Namibia. The pink to mauve flowers are produced in October–December.

Rhigozum obovatum, wild pomegranate. Family Bignoniaceae. This spiny shrub grows up to 1.2 m in height, on the shale on dry slopes in the Klein Karoo and east to the Eastern Cape, and north to the Great Karoo. Its bright yellow flowers appear July–December.

Berkheya francisci. Family Asteraceae. A shrub that grows to more than 1 m in height on the upper slopes of the Swartberg range. Its yellow flowers appear from December to January.

Babiana sp. nov. Family Iridaceae. 'Species novae' means that this is a recently discovered plant which has not yet officially been named. It is a bulb-like plant, up to 20 cm in height, and found in stony ground around De Rust. Its blue-mauve flowers appear in spring.

Tritonia securigera. Family Iridaceae. A bulb-like plant, 15–40 cm in height, bearing orange or yellow flowers with large calluses on the flower parts. It grows on hills and flats in the Klein Karoo, and across to George and the eastern Cape. The flowers are produced in September–November.

Leucadendron dregei, summit conebush. Family Proteaceae. A sprawling, 0.6-m tall shrub with a single stem and separate male and female plants. It grows in scattered fashion on the Swartberg's southern slopes (at 1 500 – 2 000 m). Status: rare. Flowers November–December.

Sutherlandia frutescens, cancer bush, or kankerbos. Family Fabaceae. A shrub that reaches up to 1 m in height, and grows throughout the dry parts of southern Africa. It has tiny grey leaflets, and scarlet flowers that are produced in July–December.

Leucadendron comosum ssp. **comosum**, ridge-cone conebush. Family Proteaceae. A shrub that grows up to 1.7 m tall in dense stands on the southern Cape mountains. Both male and female plants bear red flowers in a cone-like cluster surrounded by pale green or yellow bracts. Flowers October–November.

Nivenia binata. Family Iridaceae. This shrub grows up to 45 cm in height on the southern slopes of the Swartberg range, from Ladismith across to the Oudtshoorn areas. Its deep-blue flowers appear mainly in August–October.

Protea aristata, Ladismith sugar-bush. Family Proteaceae. A stocky shrub (2.5 m tall, 3 m across) that grows as scattered plants on rocky sandstone slopes, at altitudes of 750–2 000 m, on the Klein Swartberg. Crimson, bell-shaped flowerheads appear from October to February, though mainly in December.

Erica maximiliani. Family Ericaceae. This shrub grows on mountain ranges from the Cederberg and Langeberg and into the Klein Karoo, where it is found on the Klein Swartberg and Swartberg ranges. Its pale green to sulphur-yellow flowers appear September–December.

Protea repens, common sugar-bush. Family Proteaceae. A tall (4.5-m) shrub, widely distributed across the region. Flowerheads, which range from cream to green to red, appear in May–October in the western areas, September–March in the east.

The Garden Route

One of many attractive 'pansy' shells –
of the sea-urchin *Echindiscus* – *found in
Knysna Lagoon and along the coast.*

*A*n early French traveller, Francois le Vallaint, was full of praise for the charms of what we now call the Garden Route. 'The flowers that grow there in their millions', he wrote in the 1780s, '... make one stop and think that Nature has made an enchanted abode of this beautiful place.' Much has changed since then; farms, towns, villages, holiday resorts have transformed the countryside and its shoreline, but the essence – the shape and character of the land and, in many places, the plants that grow on it – remains intact.

The Garden Route stretches from the Slangrivier (near Heidelberg) in the west to the Storms River in the east, a 300-km belt that takes in a lovely shoreline of bays, beaches and river estuaries, a green and pleasant coastal terrace, and the high and handsome backing mountains. These last, the eastern Langeberg, the Outeniqua and the Tsitsikamma ranges, are well watered, the lower slopes graced by the subcontinent's largest (and among its last) montane forests – extensive patches of stinkwood, and giant yellowwood, ironwood, beech, assegai, candlewood, white elder and around 80 other hardwoods. Their canopies, dense though they are, allow some sunlight to filter through to the forest floor: enough to sustain a fantasia of fern, shrub, herb, lichen and moss. The highlands also have their wildlife (though it tends to be elusive): leopard, bushbuck, bushpig, baboon and a host of smaller mammals – together with some exquisite birds, among them the Knysna loerie and narina trogon – find sanctuary in the forest depths. The Garden Route is home to around 2 500 fynbos species.

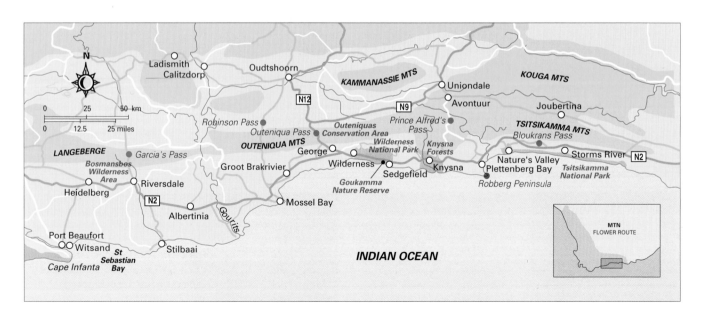

HEIDELBERG TO MOSSEL BAY

The main N2 highway takes you eastwards, along the southern flanks of the Langeberg, through the peaceful little towns of Heidelberg, Riversdale and Albertina. This is largely wheat and wool country, fairly intensively farmed – but much remains to delight the lover of nature.

Sprawling across the Langeberg's slopes are the pristine forest patches and mountain fynbos of the Boosmansbos Wilderness Area, of the adjoining, much smaller Grootvadersbosch Conservation Area, and of the Garcia State Forest. To the south lie the attractive coastal villages of Witsand, at the mouth of the Breede River, and Stilbaai, known for its fine beaches, its scenic hinterland, and its conservation areas. Indeed Stilbaai boasts an impressive number of nature reserves, among them the smallish Pauline Bohnen and Geelkrans havens and, somewhat farther to the east, Rein's Gouriqua, a privately run, 3 550-ha stretch of rather attractive countryside that preserves, among much else of interest, a wealth of limestone fynbos. The limestone sugarbush is spectacular in winter; the Mossel Bay pincushions are at their colourful best from April to September.

Eastwards, beyond the deep, aloe-filled gorge of the Gouritz River, is Mossel Bay, home to the pre-colonial 'Strandloper' people and welcome watering place for Diaz, da Gama and other early Portuguese navigators. One of the latter, João da Nova, built the first European-style structure in the country, a small stone chapel (of which nothing remains); another established the first 'post office' when, in 1500, he left his report under a large milkwood for collection by the next home-ward bound fleet. Others followed his example. The gnarled old tree – and much else of historical note, including displays devoted to the early Khoisan culture, to seashells and to the area's fynbos – can be seen in the town's Bartolemeu Diaz museum complex. Mossel Bay – the name is taken from the local mussels, much savoured by the early indigenous inhabitants – was once a quiet fishing village and holiday resort but, with the discovery of oil offshore, has grown considerably in recent years. Still, the beaches are as inviting as ever, the mussels as delicious, the sea kind to yachtsman and bathers.

Farther along the coast are the resort villages of Hartenbos, Little Brak River (winter-flowering aloes decorate the countryside here), and Great Brak River, set in attractive surrounds of sea and estuary. Some lovely flowering plants can be seen along the walking trail between the river and the local dam.

GEORGE AND WILDERNESS

Named after England's 18th-century monarch, situated in prosperous farming and forestry country beneath the splendour of the Outeniqua mountains and 'capital' of the Garden Route, George is a handsome, substantial town of wide, tree-lined streets, of good shops, hotels and restaurants, an airport and a fine museum. On the mountains to the north and northwest is the Outeniqua Conservation Area, a 38 000-ha patchwork of forest and mountain fynbos sanctuaries lying along the line between the dry interior and the moist coastal terrace. The north-facing slopes sustain karoo plant life; mountain fynbos graces the southern parts; among

notables is the lovely, rare red bulb *Cyrtanthus elatus*, commonly known as the George lily (a few specimens can be seen outside the town's handsome civic centre). Even rarer is the lily's pink form: it survives only in the remoter forest parts.

The eight-day, rather demanding Outeniqua Hiking Trail begins at Witfontein, just outside George. Watch out for the vivid blue pea flowers of *Psoralea affinis*, for bush-tea, bright yellow gum-leaf conebush and for handsome king proteas. Other rewarding but rather less strenuous excursions include the drive along the Seven Passes Road, the old route to the east, which makes its way through an enchanting countryside of river, woodland and fern forest; and a leisurely trip on the Outeniqua Choo-Tjoe, a vintage (Class 24), narrow-gauge steam train that plies between George and Knysna. En route it negotiates the Kaaimans River bridge (a scenically magnificent spot) to make its way through a beautiful land of lakes and lagoons.

Above: *Dense vegetation flanks the lower reaches of the Kaaimans River, whose beautiful estuary lies between George and Wilderness.*
Below: *The strikingly crested Knysna loerie, a shy resident of the region's forest.*

The village of Wilderness, at the mouth of Touw River, is at the western end of the region's Lake District, an area embracing seven large expanses of limpid water – the Wilderness Lagoon, Island Lake (these two are connected by the meandering waterway known as the Serpentine), Langvlei, Rondevlei, Swartvlei (the largest) and Groenvlei – which, together with some 10 000 ha of adjoining land set aside for conservation, comprises the Wilderness National Park. The sanctuary sustains forest with tall white stinkwood trees, flowering krantz aloes, delicate bulbs that cling to shaded cliffs, wetland reedbeds, sedges, aquatic plants, some 80 species of waterfowl, several kinds of antelope and the Cape clawless otter. The general area is well developed for tourism; the roads are excellent; there are plenty of recreational facilities; accommodation is available in hotels, resorts, guesthouses, cabins and cottages (at the park's Ebb and Flow rest camp). But, for all that, the land remains surprisingly unspoilt.

In fact Groenvlei, at the eastern end, forms part of the Goukamma Nature Reserve, a 2 230-ha expanse of coastal fynbos countryside that also takes in 14 km of shoreline, dunefield (comprising some of the country's highest vegetated dunes), beaches, one nautical mile of the sea, the Goukamma River's lower reaches and its estuary. The reserve is haven for around 220 bird species, for pockets of yellowwoods, milkwoods, bastard saffron, cherrywoods (also known as kershout) and many other trees. In autumn, massed off-white blombos flowers charm the senses with their honey scent, and the candelabras put on a magnificent show.

THE KNYSNA AREA

The attractive resort and residential town of Knysna is renowned for its lagoon, a 14-km long inlet whose sea entrance is guarded by two prominent sandstone cliffs known as The Heads. The lagoon is both a popular recreation area (sailing, scenic cruises, angling, watersports; rambling and picnicking along its rather splendid shores) and haven for a myriad living forms – among them aquatic birds, fish, prawns, crabs, and oysters.

Other attractions in the area include Knysna Quays, a lively waterfront shopping and leisure area; the local brewery (fine ale, visitors welcome); the Knysna oyster hatcheries (champagne served in the tavern); the Old Gaol complex, which embraces a maritime history section, an angling museum, art gallery and cafe; and Millwood House and Parkes Cottage, two evocative Victorian homes erected in the Knysna forest during the short-lived 1876 gold rush and, much later, transported in sections to be rebuilt in town. There is also the historic Royal Hotel, which started life in the 1840s and has played amiable host to many distinguished guests (including George Bernard Shaw).

The lagoon and something like 13 000 ha of the surrounding, beautifully forested countryside are encompassed within, and protected by, the Knysna National Lake Area. Venues of special interest to flower enthusiasts include the Pledge Nature Reserve, a 10-ha patch of pristine fynbos in the centre of town, and the privately run Featherbed Nature Reserve, on the western of the two Heads (scrub forest, coastal fynbos, and a most rewarding nature trail).

Farther afield are the Goudveld, Gouna and Diepwalle state forests and, on the road north to Avontuur, the Ysternek Nature Reserve – collectively known as the Knysna forests. Until recently Diepwalle served as home to the remnants of the celebrated Knysna elephants, last of the once-great Cape herds. There are some lovely walks beneath the dense canopies created by a variety of hardwood trees, among them enormous Outeniqua yellowwoods, black stinkwoods, white alders, black ironwoods and Cape chestnuts, the last covered in summer with scented, pale-pink, mauve-flecked flowers.

PLETTENBERG BAY AND TSITSIKAMMA

Perhaps the most fashionable of all the resort towns on South Africa's long southern seaboard, 'Plett' is a stylish, sundrenched place of upmarket holiday and residential homes, speciality shops, a fine arts and craft route, three enticing, largely wind-free beaches, an enchanting hinterland and plenty of sunshine (an average 320 days of it a year).

Above: *This shady track leads beneath the high hardwood canopy of the Gouda State Forest near Knysna.*
Below: *A view of the Wilderness coastline. The village, at the mouth of the Touw River, is set around a lagoon that forms the first link in a chain of lakes.*

Top: *Plettenberg Bay's Beacon Island and its stylish hotel-timeshare complex.*
Top right: *Hikers on the 61-km Tsitsikamma Trail which winds its way farther inland than the Otter Trail.*
Above: *The Storms River estuary, at the eastern end of the Tsitsikamma park.*

At the southern end of the bay is a 4-km long sandstone promontory called the Robberg Peninsula, the whole of which is a nature reserve proclaimed to protect the breeding sites of southern black-backed gulls, white-breasted cormorants and black oyster-catchers. It also conserves the low, scrubby coastal fynbos vegetation and thicket (candlewood, sea guarri, milkwood and blue kunibush). The 760-ha Keurbooms River Nature Reserve, a few kilometres from Plettenberg Bay, offers forest edged with keurbooms whose pinky-mauve flowers bloom in spring. There are some lovely rambles along the steep, well-treed river banks, around the estuary and on the fynbos-covered plateau above. Bird life includes African finfoot and breeding pairs of Caspian terns.

To the west lies the Tsitsikamma National Park, a narrow, 80-km long strip of shoreline and immediate hinterland stretching from the enchanting Nature's Valley eastwards to the Eersterivier resort. The land is well wooded, cut through by the many streams that flow down from the forested Tsitsikamma mountains to the north. South Africa's first and arguably best-known organized hiking route, the 41-km Otter Trail, leads along the coast from Storms River Mouth to Nature's Valley; on the way are cliffs, kloofs, estuaries, waterfalls, patches of indigenous forest, rock pools teeming with marine life, and a fynbos countryside decorated by wart-stemmed pincushions, buchu, gum-leafed conebush, narrow-leafed sugarbush and much else. The lovely seaboard from Plettenberg Bay to Tsitsikamma occupies the eastern extremity of the MTN Whale Route; giant humpback, southern right, Bryde's and, to a lesser extent, minke and killer whales can be spotted in the inshore waters during the cooler months.

Calendar

The Garden Route's seasons are less pronounced than those of other regions. Year-round rainfall ensures that there are always some plants in flower.

SPRING: flowering bulbs include freesias, uintjies and *Moraea*; watsonias in shades of pink along roadsides; gladioli; ghaukum (*Carpobrotus deliciosus*); the wart-stemmed and Outeniqua pincushions, and also keurboom.

SUMMER: Blue lily (*Agapanthus praecox*), the original of cultivars grown around the world. Also chincherinchees (*Ornithogalum*);

The Outeniqua mountain slopes host some enchanting blooms in season.

woolly-flowered *Lanaria lanata* on burnt hillsides; wild garlic; the George lily; wild iris on forest floors; satyriums; blue aristeas.

AUTUMN: The March lily (*Amaryllis belladonna*); *Haemanthus* species. March–May: *Plectranthus ecklonii* in moist, shady forest patches. March–July: red hot pokers; small brown afrikander (*Gladiolus maculatus*); pink-flowered orchid *Disa gladioliflora* high in the Outeniqua mountains; bulbous pelargoniums with pink-streaked flowers; bright yellow hibiscus blooms with dark red centres on the forest edges. Late autumn through to winter: scatterings of tiny sorrel flowers.

Late summer: *Plumbago capensis*, the popular garden plant. Summer through to late winter: *Streptocarpus rexii* in deep forest shade.

WINTER: Narrow-leafed sugarbush; suurkanol (*Chasmanthe aethiopica*); *Mimetes pauciflorus* flowers from June to August. *Erica chloroloma* brightens up the Goukamma dunes with its red flowers; white elder trees are decorated in tiny, creamy, fragrant flowers. Also yellow bietou and mauve-blue dune daisies.

For up-to-date information, call the MTN Flowerline 083 910 1028 (June to October).

Leonotis leonuris, wildedagga. Family Lamiaceae. A tall shrub, whose leaves have a pungent smell. Found from Paarl and Peninsula to Port Elizabeth and beyond to Mpumalanga; said to have medicinal value. Orange-red velvety flowers November–July. Pollinated by long-billed birds (such as the sunbird).

Plumbago auriculata, plumbago. Family Plumbaginaceae. A shrub or scrambler growing up to 2 m tall in scrub from Knysna to Port Elizabeth and eastwards. Light blue, occasionally white flowers from December–May. Well adapted to variable conditions, hence hardy and suited to a range of garden conditions.

Cyathea capensis, forest tree fern. Family Cyatheaceae. Grows up to 5 m tall in moist evergreen forests extending from the Cape, along the coast to the tropics. Lowermost leaves are tangled masses of green, later turning to brown hair-like structures. Found at low altitudes in tall, wet forests of the Knysna area.

Cyrtanthus elatus, George lily or Knysna lily. Family Amaryllidaceae. An exquisite flower, rare but still seen along streams in the forests. Glossy green leaves. Produces 6–10 large, brilliant scarlet, funnel-shaped flowers December–February. Pink form thought to be extinct in the wild, but widely cultivated in gardens.

Ceratandra grandiflora. Family Orchidaceae. A fairly robust plant up to 40 cm tall with 8 cm linear leaves. Flowerhead is dense with flowers of pale green and orange-yellow flushed with red. Grows in inland marshes and is endemic to the southern Cape. Flowers are produced October–December after fires.

Erica fourcadei. Family Ericaceae. Occurs along southern coast from Knysna to Cape St Francis. A lanky (up to 1.2 m tall) plant but near the sea it scrambles over boulders and may be only 30 cm in height. Long, tubular, 2–3 cm flowers, dull red to yellow with reddish stripes lengthwise, appear May–November.

Bonatea speciosa, moederkappie. Family Orchidaceae. Leafy, fairly robust orchid that grows up to 1m tall on the damp, shady lower slopes, usually in sandy soils in coastal scrub of forest margins. The green and white flowers, in a dense spike-like flowerhead, appear October–November.

Calodendrum capense, Cape chestnut. Family Rutaceae (citrus family). This is an ancient species, ancestor of all scented buchu scrubs in the Cape region. Pink flowers in large clusters appear, as bright splashes in the forest canopy, September–December.

Kniphofia uvaria, red hot poker. Family Asphodelaceae, and thus part of the greater lily family and related to the aloes. Grows up to 1.1 m tall. Widespread in wet sites from Namaqualand, the Cederberg to Peninsula and on to Port Elizabeth and beyond. The red flowers, becoming yellow, appear mainly October–January.

Virgilia oroboides, keurboom. Family Fabaceae (pea family). The Afrikaans name translates as 'choice tree', a reference to its gorgeous flowers. Grows up to 10 m tall along forest margins or streambanks from Peninsula to Mossel Bay, and around Keurbooms River. Pale pink flowers appear January–April.

Polygala myrtifolia, September bush. Family Polygalaceae. An erect, showy shrub or small tree 2.5 m tall, common in coastal scrub and fynbos along Garden Route but also in southwest and, in east, through to KwaZulu-Natal. Flowers intermittently throughout the year but at its best in spring and summer.

Podocarpus falcatus, Outeniqua yellowwood. Family Podocarpaceae, in the gymnosperm or cone tree group. The species, characteristically festooned with lichen, is among the most majestic of Knysna forest trees; once widely used for timber floors, ceilings etc., now highly prized for its honey colour and rarity.

Leucadendron eucalyptifolium, gum-leaf conebush. Family Proteaceae. The shrub can reach 5 m and become tree-like from single main stem. Grows on sandy flats and slopes. Frequent from Riversdale to Port Elizabeth. Male bracts yellow, silvery green in female. Flowers July–October.

Erica densifolia. Family Ericaceae. A 90-cm tall shrub with tubular flowers 2–3cm long, curved to fit the beak of its bird-pollinators. Grows on flats and middle slopes of mountains from Riversdale to Humansdorp, inland to Swartberg. Lovely two-tone flowers (red or white, with green tips) bloom September–March.

Syncarpha eximia, strawberry everlasting. Family Asteraceae (daisy family). A robust shrublet growing to just over 30 cm; bright reddish flowers appear November–March, mainly on south-facing slopes from Caledon to Uitenhage. Highly sought after in the cut-flower trade.

Dietes iridioides, wild iris. Family Iridaceae. Forms evergreen ground cover along forest streams and margins, but also found in drier sites. Wide distribution. Flowers white, sometimes tinged with blue. Blooms last for only a day. Flowers mainly from August to December.

Useful Contacts

Namaqualand Tourist Information Offices
tel:(0251) 22011;
fax:(0251) 21421; e-mail:
namakwaland@intekom.co.za

West Coast Tourism
(includes West Coast, Olifant's River Valley, Swartland and Sandveld), P.O. Box 242, Moorreesburg 7310; tel: (022) 433 2380; fax: (022) 433 2127; e-mail: wdr@mbury.new.co.

Cape Metropolitan Tourism
P.O. Box 16548, Vlaeberg 8018; tel: (021) 487 2718; fax: (021) 487 2977; e-mail: cmt@cmc.gov.za

Cape Town Tourism,
Pinnacle Building, corner of Burg and Castle streets, Cape Town, 8001; tel: (021) 426 4267/8; fax: (021) 426 4266; e-mail: captour@iafrica.com

Winelands Regional Tourism Organisation
P.O. Box 3124, Paarl 7620; tel: (021) 872 0686; fax: (021) 872 0534; e-mail: wsto@cis.co.za

Breede River Valley Tourism
P.O. Box 91, Worcester 6849; tel: (023) 347 6411; fax: (023) 347 1115; e-mail: tourism@boland.lia

Cape Overberg Tourism Association
P.O. Box 250, Caledon 7230; tel: (028) 214 1466; fax: (028) 212 1380; e-mail: cota@capeoverberg.co.za

Klein Karoo Kannaland Tourism
P.O. Box 127, Oudtshoorn 6670; tel: (044) 272 2241; fax: (044) 279 2667; e-mail: kkdr@pixie.co.za

Garden Route Regional Tourism Office
P.O. Box 1514, George 6530; tel: (044) 873 6314/55; fax: (044) 272 2241; fax: (044) 884 0688; email: info@gardenroute.org.za

Index

Photo credits

Credits read from top to bottom and then left to right. Abbreviations: SIL=Struik Image Library RDPL=Roger de la Harpe Photographic Library

Roger de la Harpe/RDPL: 76b, 82a. Nigel Dennis: 81a. Philip Desmet: 13b&e, 16g, 21b, 79b. Gerhard Dreyer: 11, 12a, 20, 21a, 23, 24/25, 61. Jean du Plessis: 55a. Ken Findlay: 71b. Gwynneth Glass: 16b&d&e&f, 17b&c&e&f, 18a, 34e, 63b, 65e, 69a.

Walter Knirr: 27. John Manning: 13d&h, 16c, 17a&d&g, 19c. Colin Paterson-Jones: 1, 2, 3, 9a-e, 13a&c&f&g, 16a, 18b&c, 19a&b&d, 25a-d, 32a-f, 33a-d, 34a-d, 34f-h, 35a-h, 37, 38b&d, 39b, 40a-g, 41a-h, 44a-h, 45, 46, 47a-h, 48a-c, 56a-g, 57a-c, 58a, 60, 63a, 64, 65a-d, 65f&g, 67, 69b, 70a-f, 73, 74a-h, 75a-h, 78, 79c&d, 82b, 83, 84a-g, 85a-h, 92a-h, 93a-h. Photo Access/P.Wagner: 88b. SIL: 42, 43. SIL/Shaen Adey: 26, 28a, 30b, 33e, 38a&c, 39a,

52a-c, 53b, 54a&b, 59, 72a, 77a&b, 80a. SIL/Nigel Dennis: 49. SIL/Gerhard Dreyer: 72b, 79a, 81b, 86, 87, 88a, 89a&b, 90a&b, 91. SIL/Anneline Oberholzer: 71a. SIL/Mark Skinner: 31a. SIL/Erhardt Thiel: 53a. SIL/Hein von Hörsten: 12b, 21c, 29, 58b, 66a &b, 80b, 90c. SIL/Lanz von Hörsten: 14, 15, 28b, 31b, 51, 55b&c, 76a. Mark Skinner: 30a. Tourism Board/Hein von Hörsten: 7, 62. Lanz von Hörsten: 68a, 82c.